Grammar
Form and Function 3B
Second Edition

WORKBOOK

Milada Broukal
Amy Parker

Mc Graw Hill Education

Grammar Form and Function, 2nd Edition 3B Workbook

English Adaptation 2011

Original ISBN: 978-0-07-310412-6

Editorial director: Tina B. Carver
Executive editor: Erik Gundersen
Senior developmental editor: Annie Sullivan
Editorial assistant: Kasey Williamson
Production manager: MaryRose Malley
Cover design: Preface, Inc.
Interior design: Preface, Inc.

Photo credits:
All photos are courtesy of Getty Images Royalty-Free Collection.

2 3 4 5 6 7 8 9 0 Artec 20 18

When ordering this title, please use

ISBN 10: 89-6055-202-X
ISBN 13: 978-89-6055-202-9

Printed in Korea

Contents

UNIT 8 THE PASSIVE VOICE, CAUSATIVES, AND PHRASAL VERBS

UNIT 9 GERUNDS AND INFINITIVES

UNIT 10 AGREEMENT AND PARALLEL STRUCTURE

UNIT 11 NOUN CLAUSES AND REPORTED SPEECH

UNIT 12 ADJECTIVE CLAUSES

UNIT 13 ADVERB CLAUSES

UNIT 14 CONDITIONAL SENTENCES

UNIT 8 THE PASSIVE VOICE, CAUSATIVES, AND PHRASAL VERBS

8a The Passive Voice: Overview

Student Book p. 220

1 Practice

Read the sentences. Write *A* next to the sentence if it is in the active voice. Write *P* if it is in the passive voice.

_____ **1.** My cousin owns a garage.

_____ **2.** Recently, I took my car there for repairs.

_____ **3.** In the past, I had been charged too much money by another garage.

_____ **4.** In addition, other damages to the car were caused by those mechanics.

_____ **5.** My car was fixed by my cousin himself.

_____ **6.** However, I was shocked when I saw the bill.

_____ **7.** I had been charged even more money by my cousin!

_____ **8.** I wasn't given a family discount at all!

2 Practice

Read the sentences. Write *N* next to the sentence if the agent (with a *by* phrase) is needed because it is important to the writer's meaning. Write *U* if the agent is unnecessary or unimportant.

_____ **1.** Camera film is made by the Cameramatics Company.

_____ **2.** The company was founded in 1961 by a man named Leonard Jameson.

_____ **3.** Recently, the company's sales have been hurt by the increase in sales of digital cameras.

_____ **4.** Digital cameras are being used more often by people.

_____ **5.** Thirty-five millimeter cameras are gradually being replaced by digital cameras.

_____ **6.** In digital cameras, photos are saved on small disks by people.

_____ **7.** At Cameramatics, 200 employees were laid off by Mr. Jameson last month.

_____ **8.** A hundred more employees are going to be dismissed by the new manager next month.

_____ **9.** Many other changes have been made by the company's executives lately.

_____ **10.** A new marketing strategy will be announced by the marketing department at the end of the week.

3 Practice

Rewrite the following paragraphs in the passive voice where appropriate. State the agent in a *by* phrase only when necessary. Use the correct verb tense and change object/subject pronouns if necessary.

A.

Welcome to Island Tours! We have a few guidelines to give you. First, we request passengers to carry their identification at all times. We also expect passengers to take their boarding passes with them whenever they leave the boat. If anyone loses their boarding pass, we will charge them a $15.00 replacement fee. Finally, we ask passengers to be very careful on the upper deck. Deck hands have just washed the upper deck. The wood is very slippery right now.

____

____

____

____

____

____

____

____

____

____

B.

Yesterday, Lars Larsen won the cross-country skiing championship. This is the third year that the champion skier from Norway has won the race. But two days ago, no one believed Lars would win this race. He had injured his left knee six months before the big event. He had surgery on that knee in October. Early in this race, the knee injury troubled Lars. Many people thought he was going to drop out of the race. However, thousands of fans in Norway encouraged Lars. Hundreds of people came all the way to Utah to support him in this race. Lars said that his fans motivated him to win. After a while, he forgot the pain. He passed a rival skier, Italy's Marco Bernini. Once again, the race officials awarded Lars the Golden Ski.

C.

Major floods have destroyed much of Watertown, Ohio. The problems began last week when heavy rains raised the water level in the river. In addition, construction in the area had already damaged the river wall. The town made great efforts to stop the flooding. People built walls out of sandbags all along the river. But the rains continued, and the river water continued to rise and move towards the town. People boarded up windows of homes and businesses. They moved important belongings to the rooftops. Eventually, most residents vacated homes. The National Guard relocated people to shelters in nearby towns. Helicopters took some people from their rooftops and flew them to the shelters. The flood caused nearly $3 million in damage. The town will request emergency aid from federal funds.

____

8b The Passive Voice of Modals and Modal Phrases

Student Book p. 226

4 Practice

Read about Mrs. Ellis. Complete the sentences with the words in parentheses and the passive modal or passive perfect modal. Pay attention to time words and phrases. Some sentences refer to the past, some refer to the present, and others refer to the future.

1. In the evenings, our elderly neighbor, Mrs. Ellis, (can, find) *can be found* watching TV in her living room.
2. She (can, see) ____________ eating alone and looking at old photographs.
3. We think her family (should, tell) ____________ that she needs help in order to live on her own.
4. They (ought to, inform) ____________ about this problem a long time ago.
5. The grass outside of Mrs. Ellis's house (has to, cut) ____________ soon; it is very tall and full of weeds.
6. The garbage bins by the garage (must, empty) ____________.
7. They (must not, empty) ____________ for a month or more.
8. The windows and curtains (ought to, wash) ____________.
9. In fact, they (ought to, wash) ____________ last spring.
10. When we talked to Mrs. Ellis yesterday, she said her carpets (be supposed to, clean) ____________ last week, but the cleaning service never arrived.
11. She also said the telephone company (has to, pay) ____________ a while ago, but she couldn't find her checkbook.
12. She worried that her phone service (could, disconnect) ____________ next month if she doesn't pay her bill.
13. I hope Mrs. Ellis's family (will, inform) ____________ about these problems in the near future.
14. Otherwise, I think Mrs. Ellis (had better, move) ____________ to a different home where people can help her live independently.

5 Practice

Read the sentences. Write *C* next to the sentence if the passive modal is used correctly. Write *I* if it is used incorrectly.

______ **1.** This mess had better clean by this time tomorrow.

______ **2.** You are going to be charged for the doctor's appointment that you missed.

______ **3.** The rules of the road must obeyed by all drivers.

______ **4.** The homework should had been returned today, but the teacher hadn't finished grading it.

______ **5.** The job might be given to someone with more experience.

______ **6.** Yesterday's soccer game had to cancelled because of the rain.

______ **7.** The order might be shipped as early as Wednesday.

______ **8.** The plane can't been delayed by weather; the weather was perfect in Florida today.

8c The Passive Voice with *Get; Get* + Adjective

Student Book p. 229

6 Practice

Read about Rosa. Use *get* + words from the list to complete the missing information. Use the correct tense. Use "delivered" twice.

bored	involved
delivered	married
depressed	older
divorced	scared
excited	tired
exhibited	worried
hurt	younger at heart

My great-aunt Rosa just turned 80, but she isn't sad about it. In fact, she never *gets depressed* (1). She says that while she ____________ (2) in actual years, she also ______________ (3). She has friends who stopped being interested in new things when they turned 70. They stopped exercising, and as a result, their energy level went down — they ______________ (4) more easily. Rosa says that if people don't try to stay interested and involved in life's activities, they ______________ (5) in their later years. In contrast, Aunt Rosa ______________ (6) about the next decade of her life. To celebrate her birthday, she bought a motor scooter. Her children ______________ (7) when Rosa first told them that she wanted to buy a scooter. They ______________ (8) that she would have an accident and that she would ______________ (9). Rosa was never scared. The only time she worried was when the scooter did not ______________ (10) on time.

What else does Rosa do to stay active? Just recently, she ______________ (11) with a hiking group for seniors. She also works with an organization that helps children with cancer. She makes teddy bears that ______________ (12) to children in hospitals all over the world. She makes pottery, and some of her work ______________ (13) at an arts and crafts show next month. She enjoys the company of her new husband. She ______________ (14) last year, at age 79! Before that, she had been married for thirty years, but she and her previous husband ______________ (15).

7 Practice

Look back at the numbered sentences in Practice 6. Write *B* for the sentences in which *get* means *become*. Write *O* for sentences with other meanings of *get*.

1. B	6. ____	11. ____
2. ____	7. ____	12. ____
3. ____	8. ____	13. ____
4. ____	9. ____	14. ____
5. ____	10. ____	15. ____

8 Practice

Write at least four sentences about each emotion pictured. Use *get* + an adjective in the present: what do you do when you have this emotion? Then use *get* + an adjective in the past. Write about a time when you had this emotion. What happened?

Example: *I get anxious when I have to speak in public.*
When I get worried about that, I bite my nails.
I got really scared once when I was in a school play.

1. ____

____

____

____

____

2. ____

____

____

____

____

3. ____

____

____

____

____

8d *It* + a Passive Voice Verb + a *That* Clause

Student Book p. 233

9 Practice

Rewrite the sentences in two ways. The first time, use *it* + a passive voice verb + a *that* clause. The second time, use the subject of the active *that* clause as the subject of another passive sentence.

1. People say that my friend Luke is a genius.

   It is said that my friend Luke is a genius.

   My friend Luke is said to be a genius.

2. The newspaper reported that his software company is the most successful new business of the year.

   ____

   ____

3. Economists estimate that his sales will double next month.

   ____

   ____

4. Consumers believe his products are changing people's lives.

   ____

   ____

5. Everyone knows that starting a new business is difficult in today's economy.

   ____

   ____

6. People think Luke is especially successful because he is only twenty-seven!

   ____

   ____

10 Practice

Write six sentences with *it* + a passive voice verb + a *that* clause. Choose from verbs in the list.

believe	fear	report
confirm	hope	think
consider	know	
estimate	mention	

Example: war
It is feared that this war will not end soon.

1. teenagers today

____

2. the planet Mars

____

3. college

____

4. cigarettes

____

5. movies

____

6. yoga

____

8e Present and Past Participles Used as Adjectives

Student Book p. 235

11 Practice

Read the movie review. Circle the correct adjectives in parentheses.

REVIEW: Danger Zone a Bore ★☆☆☆☆

The new movie *Danger Zone* was supposed to be the blockbuster of the summer, but it was (disappointed / disappointing)[1]. In fact, I felt so (disappointed / disappointing)[2] by it that I almost walked out before it ended! First of all, the movie — despite its (exciting / excited)[3] title — is really very (bored / boring)[4]. Nothing happens for the first twenty minutes of the movie. Then the story gets (confused / confusing)[5] when we are suddenly introduced to four new characters. These characters seem (interested / interesting) [6] at first because they are all very different from each other. But I was (surprising / surprised) [7] when the characters went away, never to be seen again. The special effects in the movie are (impressive / impressed) [8]. Clearly a lot of money was spent on this part of the film. The car chase that went from the streets of New York into outer space was (amazing / amazed) [9], although it went on a bit too long. By the end of that scene, I was actually (amusing / amused) [10], but I think the director wanted the audience to feel (frightening / frightened) [11]. The worst part of the movie is that it is over two hours long. It was (exhausted / exhausting) [12] to watch the whole thing from beginning to end. I think they could have cut ninety minutes off of this movie, and it might have been more (interested / interesting) [13] as a result. It certainly wouldn't have been as (tired / tiring) [14] to watch!

12 Practice

Write about a time in your life when you felt confused, embarrassed, exhausted, or relaxed. Use at least eight present and past participle adjectives. You may tell your story in the past or the present.

Example: *On my first day of classes at my new school, I was very confused. I couldn't understand my schedule, and I was embarrassed when I went to the wrong class. The map of the school was also confusing, and I got lost several times...*

____

____

____

____

____

____

____

____

8f Causative Sentences with *Have, Get,* and *Make:* Active Voice

Student Book p. 237

13 Practice

Gloria and her new roommate, Alison, disagree about what they should have done to the apartment. Read their conversation. Rewrite the causative sentences using *have, make,* or *get* and the words in parentheses. Pay attention to tenses. More than one answer may be possible.

Alison: White walls are depressing. My brother is a painter. I think we should (my brother, paint) *have my brother paint* (OR) *get my brother to paint* them purple and blue. I (him, paint) ______(2)______ my last apartment, and it looked great. He would be happy to do it for us.

Gloria: The landlord won't let us paint the walls. We'll never (him, agree) ______(3)______ to it. I'm sure he would (us, repaint) ______(4)______ the walls white.

Alison: Did these curtains come with the apartment? I have a friend who's an interior designer. I'd like to (her, replace) ______(5)______ them with newer ones.

Gloria: My mother made those curtains for me. I like them. I can't (her, take) ______(6)______ them down.

Alison: Do you think we can (the neighbors, move) ______(7)______ those bicycles off of their balcony? They aren't very nice to look at.

Gloria: I don't think so. Their bikes were stolen last year. They (the landlord, give) ______(8)______ them permission to keep their bikes there.

Alison: I don't like cleaning. I think we should (a housekeeper, clean) ______(9)______ the apartment once a week.

Gloria: I can't afford it. I've never (anyone, clean) ______(10)______ my apartment for me.

Alison: I'll pay for it. I'll (you, see) ______(11)______ how much nicer it is to (someone else, do) ______(12)______ the work!

8g Causative Sentences with *Have* and *Get:* Passive Voice

Student Book p. 241

14 Practice

Use the prompts to write one causative sentence in the passive voice with *get* or *have*. Then rewrite the sentence in the active voice (See section 8f, Student Book p. 21). Use the tense specified and pay attention to the structure with *get* in the active voice.

1. simple present: I / always / prescriptions / fill / same pharmacy

a. *I always get/have my prescriptions filled at the same pharmacy.*

b. *I always get the same pharmacy to fill my prescriptions.*

(OR) *I always have the same pharmacy fill my prescriptions.*

2. present perfect: Linda / her résumé / edit / a career counselor / a few times this year

a. ______________________________.

b. ______________________________.

3. present progressive: Noel / checks / cash / bank

a. ______________________________.

b. ______________________________.

4. simple present: James / usually / hair / cut / a family friend

a. ______________________________.

b. ______________________________.

5. simple past: Sandy / nails / paint / her favorite manicurist / last Friday

a. ______________________________.

b. ______________________________.

6. modal: Rachel / should / teeth / look at / the dentist / soon

a. ______________________________.

b. ______________________________.

7. present perfect: Midge / her cat / just / check / Dr. Neuman

a. ______________________________

______________________________.

b. ______________________________

______________________________.

8. simple past: Maryam / laundry / do / the laundromat / last week

a. ______________________________.

b. ______________________________.

9. future with *will:* I / will / my apartment / redecorate / an interior designer / next summer

a. ______________________________.

b. ______________________________.

10. present progressive: Ellen / film editing program/ explain / Marcus

a. ______________________________

______________________________.

b. ______________________________

______________________________.

15 Practice

What things would you get someone to do for you, or have done for you, if you were in these situations? What would you NOT have done for you? Write two sentences for each of the following situations, one positive and one negative.

Example: *If I were very wealthy, I would get someone else to do my hair and makeup for me.*
I wouldn't have bodyguards follow me around.

1. if you were very wealthy

______________________________.

______________________________.

2. if you were 100 years old

____.

____.

3. if you were a famous movie star

____.

____.

4. if you were a parent of quintuplets (five babies at once)

____.

____.

5. if you were the teacher of this class

____.

____.

8h Phrasal Verbs

Student Book p. 243

16 Practice

Complete the sentences with particles from the list. You'll use them more than once.

about	on
across	out
down	over
into	up
off	with

Jason and Tina have been dating for almost a year, but last week they nearly broke ___*up*___ (1) when they went on a long bike ride together. They had been planning this trip for months, working ____________ (2) in the gym to prepare for the 100-mile ride. But the day of the big ride, Jason showed ____________ (3) late to pick ____________ (4) Tina at her house.

On the way to the starting point of the big ride, they ran ________ (5) a friend who said it was supposed to rain. Sure enough, as soon as they showed ________ (6) at the starting point of the ride, they learned that the ride might be called ________ (7) or put ________ (8) because of the weather. Jason and Tina realized they had left ________ (9) their rain gear when they packed their bags. At last, it stopped raining, and the riders took ________ (10).

About ten miles into the ride, Tina's tire hit a rock, and she fell ________ (11). When Jason helped her get ________ (12), she realized her knee was hurting. She didn't want to give ________ (13) after they had worked so hard to get there, so she put a bandage ________ (14) her knee and went ________ (15). Ten miles later, Jason's bike broke ________ (16). He used his cell phone to call ________ (17) a bike mechanic for help.

By this time, all the other riders had passed them. They looked ________ (18) the map to make sure they were going the right way. But soon they realized they were lost. Jason started to complain. Tina told him to get ________ (19) it; that there was nothing they could do. Maybe someone would give them a ride. Maybe they could get dropped ________ (20) at the starting point. She said she couldn't put up ________ (21) his complaining anymore. Jason told her she should just finish the ride herself. Tina told him to grow ________ (22).

Then they agreed to stop arguing and to ride a few miles more. They came ________ (23) a road with a sign directing the bicyclists. They went ________ (24) the road and found other bicyclists. When they finally finished the 100-mile ride, they were so happy that they forgot they had thought ________ (25) quitting!

17 Practice

Reread the sentences in Practice 16. Write *S* if the phrasal verb is separable. Write *I* if it is inseparable.

1. I
2. ____
3. ____
4. ____
5. ____
6. ____
7. ____
8. ____
9. ____
10. ____
11. ____
12. ____
13. ____
14. ____
15. ____
16. ____
17. ____
18. ____
19. ____
20. ____
21. ____
22. ____
23. ____
24. ____
25. ____

18 Practice

Rewrite each sentence two ways. Use appropriate pronouns if necessary. If the sentence cannot be rewritten because the phrasal verb is inseparable, write *inseparable verb.*

1. John picked Emily up after work.

   John picked her up after work.

   John picked up Emily after work.

2. They are going to tear down that old building.

   ____________________.

   ____________________.

3. Everyone stood up while the national anthem was sung.

   ____________________.

   ____________________.

4. Where should I drop off the books?

   ____________________?

   ____________________?

5. I don't know how to set up my new computer.

____.

____.

6. When the war broke out, many families left the country.

____.

____.

7. Somebody used up all the sugar.

____.

____.

8. Let's get dressed up and go into the city!

____.

____.

8i Prepositions Following Verbs, Adjectives, and Nouns; Other Combinations with Prepositions

Student Book p. 248

19 Practice

Complete the sentences with phrases and expressions from the list.

according to	disappointed with	impact on	shouting at
complained about	essential to	need for	solution to
contribute to	fight for	opposed to	tired of
cost of	fond of	responsible for	

Teenagers and their parents in our neighborhood have spoken of a ___need for___(1) a community center for young people. Such a center would greatly ______________(2) the health and growth of our community. Right now, many young people are ______________(3) the town. They feel that there isn't anywhere for them to go after school or on weekends. They are ______________(4) going to the local fast-food place, and the people in the community aren't very

_______________ seeing them there all the time either. Local merchants
5

have _______________ the large number of young people that wander up
6

and down the street. They are always _______________ them to move
7

away from their stores or to go somewhere else.

One _______________ this problem would be to build a teen
8

center. _______________ studies in social psychology, teens that have
9

somewhere to go and regularly scheduled activities feel more positive about their lives. Teens participating in activities at a center also learn positive ways to make an

_______________ a community and to create positive change in
10

their world.

Of course, the _______________ a teen center isn't cheap. And
11

who would be _______________ paying those costs? We would. Now, it's
12

true that many people may be _______________ the idea of using their
13

tax dollars to build this center. But a teen center is _______________
14

the well-being of our young people, and it is something that we should

_______________.
15

SELF-TEST

A Choose the best answer, A, B, C, or D, to complete the sentence. Mark your answer by darkening the oval with the same letter.

1. He went to the garage to ___________.

A. have his car repaired Ⓐ Ⓑ Ⓒ Ⓓ
B. have to repair his car
C. make his car repaired
D. his car have repaired

2. The family ___________ when they heard a noise downstairs.

A. got scared Ⓐ Ⓑ Ⓒ Ⓓ
B. getting scared
C. got scarey
D. gets scared

3. Which is the passive causative sentence?

A. Dr. Battaglia has just vaccinated Maria's dogs. Ⓐ Ⓑ Ⓒ Ⓓ
B. Maria has just had Dr. Battaglia vaccinate her dogs.
C. Maria has just gotten her dogs vaccinated by Dr. Battaglia.
D. Maria has just gotten Dr. Battaglia to vaccinate her dogs.

4. The taxi ___________ by a famous actor.

A. driven Ⓐ Ⓑ Ⓒ Ⓓ
B. drove
C. be driven
D. was driven

5. The teacher ___________ be quiet.

A. couldn't made the students Ⓐ Ⓑ Ⓒ Ⓓ
B. couldn't make the students
C. couldn't the students make
D. couldn't to make the students

6. All customers ___________ that the store is closing next month.

A. will tell Ⓐ Ⓑ Ⓒ Ⓓ
B. are going to tell
C. been told
D. will be told

7. ___________ my father, I would like to accept this award in his name.

A. In behalf of Ⓐ Ⓑ Ⓒ Ⓓ
B. Of behalf
C. On behalf of
D. With behalf of

8. She ___________ whenever she reads the newspaper.

A. gets depressed Ⓐ Ⓑ Ⓒ Ⓓ
B. depressing
C. be depressed
D. depressed

9. Don't ___________ any longer; it's due tomorrow morning.

A. the homework put off Ⓐ Ⓑ Ⓒ Ⓓ
B. put off the homework
C. off put the homework
D. put the homework

10. Katrina ___________ her blood pressure tomorrow.

A. is getting her doctor check Ⓐ Ⓑ Ⓒ Ⓓ
B. is having her doctor to check
C. is getting her doctor to check
D. is having checked

B Find the underlined word or phrase, A, B, C, or D, that is incorrect. Mark your answer by darkening the oval with the same letter.

1. It is said (A) that students learn more when (B) they are interesting (C) in (D) the subject.

Ⓐ Ⓑ Ⓒ Ⓓ

2. Because so many (A) students failed (B), the exam given (C) again by the teachers (D).

Ⓐ Ⓑ Ⓒ Ⓓ

3. The plane wasn't arrived (A) on time (B) because there were (C) snowstorms in the Midwest (D).

Ⓐ Ⓑ Ⓒ Ⓓ

4. She couldn't concentrate (A) in (B) her work with all the irritating (C) noise in the room (D).

Ⓐ Ⓑ Ⓒ Ⓓ

5. We tried to get (A) refunded our money (B), but (C) we weren't successful at (D) it.

Ⓐ Ⓑ Ⓒ Ⓓ

6. This piece must (A) had been (B) painted (C) by a famous and talented (D) artist.

Ⓐ Ⓑ Ⓒ Ⓓ

7. All employees should (A) informed (B) about (C) the new rules and go over (D) the handbook.

Ⓐ Ⓑ Ⓒ Ⓓ

8. It is believed (A) that (B) most car accidents happen (C) when drivers get tire (D).

Ⓐ Ⓑ Ⓒ Ⓓ

9. We were surprised (A) and worried (B) when the police made (C) us to leave (D) the building.

Ⓐ Ⓑ Ⓒ Ⓓ

10. The winner will been (A) notified next week (B) and told (C) where to pick up the prize (D).

Ⓐ Ⓑ Ⓒ Ⓓ

UNIT 9 GERUNDS AND INFINITIVES

9a Gerunds as Subjects and Objects; Verbs Followed by Gerunds

Student Book p. 264

1 Practice

Write *G* next to the sentence if the underlined word is a gerund. Write *V* if the underlined word is a verb.

_____ **1.** Learning a new language takes a lot of effort and practice.

_____ **2.** I am taking French classes at a language school.

_____ **3.** For me, speaking French is very difficult.

_____ **4.** I really enjoy writing in French.

_____ **5.** Practicing French is difficult because I can't find people to speak it with.

_____ **6.** Recently, however, I have been practicing French with a friend from my class.

_____ **7.** We are trying to talk in French for an hour every week.

_____ **8.** I can't wait to go shopping in France someday and use my French there!

2 Practice

Complete the sentences with the gerund form of verbs from the list.

be	give up	learn	snowboard	swim
exercise	go	ride	stand	take
fall	keep	ski	surf	travel

My friends recently persuaded me to go __snowboarding__ (1) with them up in the mountains. I didn't want to go. I can't stand ______________ (2) cold. I like warm weather and water sports, so I prefer going ______________ (3) in a pool or ______________ (4) in the ocean. Also, I had never even gone ______________ (5) before, so I could not imagine ______________ (6) down a mountain with my feet strapped to a single piece of wood!

Nevertheless, last weekend I found myself ______ (7) up to the mountains with my friends. They said that ______ (8) a private lesson was the best way to learn how to snowboard. ______ (9) my balance on the board was hard, and ______ (10) down over and over again was painful. I considered ______ (11). However, by the end of the day, I was standing on the board and going down small hills by myself. I realized that ______ (12) on a snowboard wasn't that different from ______ (13) a surfboard. I enjoyed ______ (14) how to do a new sport, but I think I still enjoy ______ (15) in the warm weather more!

3 Practice

Circle the correct form of the words in parentheses.

Sofia enjoys (reads / reading) (1) Harry Potter novels. She couldn't resist (buying / buy) (2) the latest one as soon as it was (publishing / published) (3). She has almost (finishing / finished) (4) the most recent book, but she doesn't (wanting / want) (5) to finish it. She can't imagine (leave / leaving) (6) the characters of Harry, Hermione, and Ron and (wait / waiting) (7) until the next book to find out what happens. (Discuss / Discussing) (8) the Harry Potter novels with her friends is one of Sofia's favorite things to do.

They are always (argue / arguing) about which book is the best. Tonight they are all
9

(go / going) to see the newest Harry Potter movie. People say that this movie (is / being)
10 11

even better than the last one. Sofia (enjoys / enjoying) the Harry Potter movies, but she
12

prefers (read / reading) the books. She also (hoping / hopes) that the author,
13 14

J. K. Rowling, will keep on (writing / write) these novels. She can't imagine not
15

(read / reading) about the continuing adventures of Harry and his friends.
16

4 Practice

Use each of the following gerunds as the subject of a sentence about yourself or about people you know. Then use each gerund as the object in a sentence.

Example: **a.** (subject) *Dancing is difficult for my boyfriend.*

b. (object) *My boyfriend doesn't enjoy dancing very much.*

1. dancing

a. ______________________________

b. ______________________________

2. listening (to)

a. ______________________________

b. ______________________________

3. studying

a. ______________________________

b. ______________________________

4. traveling

a. ______________________________

b. ______________________________

5. watching

a. ______________________________

b. ______________________________

6. cooking

a. ______________________________

b. ______________________________

9b Gerunds as Objects of Prepositions; Gerunds after Certain Expressions

Student Book p. 268

5 Practice

Read the sentences and circle the correct prepositions in parentheses.

1. My friends and I are looking forward (in / at / to) having our spring break.
2. We plan (in / on / to) going to Four Flags Amusement Park.
3. Most of us are interested (on / in / about) going on the new roller coaster there.
4. However, one of our friends, Kim, says that the ride will be a waste (in / at / of) time and money.
5. Kim heard that the lines for the roller coaster are very long, so she says there's no point (in / of / for) standing in a long line to go on a short ride.
6. However, she won't stop us (for / on / from) going on the ride if we want to.
7. She has plans (in / for / on) going shopping while we wait in line for the ride.
8. She says she isn't good (at / in / on) standing in line in the hot sun.

6 Practice

Describe yourself as a student. Answer the questions using gerunds after the prepositions and expressions. Write your answers in complete sentences.

Example: *These days I am busy studying for the TOEFL.*

1. What are you busy doing these days?

   ____

2. What do you have difficulty doing?

   ____

3. What don't you have trouble doing?

   ____

4. What else are you good at doing?

   ____

5. What are you tired of doing?

____

6. What do you think is a waste of time doing?

____

7. Has a teacher ever stopped you from doing something? What was it?

____

8. What is something you look forward to doing soon?

____

9c Verbs Followed by Infinitives

Student Book p. 271

7 Practice

Mrs. Torres is leaving for work. Her husband and son are saying goodbye. Rewrite the sentences using the verbs in parentheses. Remember that some verbs need objects and some pronouns may need to change. In some cases, more than one answer may be possible.

1. Mr. Torres said, "I'll make breakfast for Alex." (agree)

   Mr. Torres agreed to make breakfast for Alex.

2. Mrs. Torres said, "Alex, don't forget to brush your teeth after breakfast." (remind)

   ____

3. Alex said, "Please bring me a picture of your office, Mom." (ask)

   ____

4. Mrs. Torres said, "Be good and do everything your father asks." (tell)

   ____

5. Alex said, "Please come home early." (want)

   ____

6. Mrs. Torres said, "I'll call you and Dad at lunch." (promise)

____

7. Alex said, "Maybe I can watch TV while Mommy is at work!" (hope)

____

8. Mrs. Torres said to her husband, "Don't let him watch more than one hour of TV." (warn, not)

____

9. Mr. Torres said to his wife, "You'll be back home by 5:30, right?" (expect)

____

10. Mrs. Torres said, "Call Kevin next door if you need any help." (encourage)

____

8 Practice

Read the sentences. Write *C* next to the sentence if an infinitive is used correctly. Write *I* if it is used incorrectly.

_____ **1.** The sign warned people to walk not on the grass.

_____ **2.** Her parents didn't permit her to date boys until she was eighteen.

_____ **3.** The neighbors threatened to called the police about the noise.

_____ **4.** Mr. Johnson was asked to move his car, but he refused do it.

_____ **5.** Can you manage to move all those boxes by yourself, or do you want someone to help you?

_____ **6.** We invited him to come on the camping trip, but his parents wouldn't allow him to go.

_____ **7.** Students who can't afford pay the tuition are advised apply for financial aid.

_____ **8.** Some colleges encourage students studying in another country for one semester or longer.

9d Verbs Followed by a Gerund or an Infinitive

Student Book p. 273

9 Practice

Hannah and Joseph are driving to a national park and have gotten lost. Read their conversation. Circle the correct form of the words in parentheses. Circle both forms if they mean the same thing.

Hannah: I think we should continue (driving / to drive)[1] until we find a gas station. When we find one, we can stop (asking / to ask)[2] for directions to the national park.

Joseph: We don't need to stop (driving / to drive)[3]. I don't like (asking / to ask)[4] for directions – I'm sure we've just made a simple mistake. We should try (reading / to read)[5] this map and figure out where we are.

Hannah: I regret (telling / to tell)[6] you that you're looking at the wrong map. I forgot (bringing / to bring)[7] the Vermont map with us. This is a map of another state.

Joseph: Then I guess we'll have to remember (planning / to plan)[8] our trip back in April. Do you recall what road we were supposed to take?

Hannah: No. But now I think I know what happened. We forgot (getting / to get)[9] off the highway at Exit 24.

Joseph: I remember (seeing / to see)[10] the sign for Exit 24. But that was about fifteen miles back! This is why I hate (traveling / to travel)[11] in such rural areas.

10 Practice

Complete the email message with the gerund or infinitive form of the words in parentheses. In some cases, either a gerund or an infinitive may be possible.

I'm in a play! - Message

Send Save Insert File... Priority Options...

To... mls1@marksmith.com

Cc...

Subject: I'm in a play!

Dear Uncle Mark,

You know how much I enjoy (act) ___acting___ (1). You always encouraged me (take) _______________ (2) drama classes. And you were the one who persuaded me (try) _______________ (3) for a part in a play. I've worked very hard, and at times I didn't think I was good at (act) _______________ (4). In fact, there were times I wanted to stop (act) _______________ (5) and do something else with my time. Well, I have good news! Now I don't regret (spend) _______________ (6) so much of my time on acting. I have a part in the school play!

It's not a big role. I don't come onstage until Act 2. But in one important scene, I pretend (be) _______________ (7) very sick. In another scene, I say an important line, and then I continue (stand) _______________ (8) on stage for about two minutes. I look forward to (rehearse) _______________ (9) the play. I expect (learn) _______________ (10) a lot about the theater from this experience. I'm not very good at (remember) _______________ (11) lines, but I will try (do) _______________ (12) my best and remember them. I hope I remember (say) _______________ (13) all my lines correctly!

Oh, I almost forgot (tell) _______________ (14) you . . . I would really like (invite) _______________ (15) you to the opening night of my play. I hope (see) _______________ (16) you there!

Your niece,

Katira

9e Infinitives after Certain Adjectives, Nouns, and Indefinite Pronouns

Student Book p. 276

11 Practice

Complete the sentences with the infinitive form of verbs from the list.

borrow	have	run
do	hear	stop
drive	let	tell
find	pick up	visit
go	practice	

Jenna: I passed my driving test and got my license! And I'm proud _to tell_ (1) you that I got an almost perfect score!

Mother: I'm so pleased ____________ (2) that, honey.

Jenna: So can I borrow the car this afternoon? I have some friends ____________ (3).

Mother: I know you're eager ____________ (4). But I'm not sure you're ready to take the car by yourself. I'm hesitant ____________ (5) you take the car on the busy roads. I think it's important for you ____________ (6) more first.

Jenna: Please? I'll be careful ____________ (7) only on quiet streets. I'm not likely ____________ (8) a lot of traffic on Belmont Street.

Mother: I don't know. I think this weekend is a better time for you ______(9)______ the car. I have some things ______(10)______ this afternoon, and I need the car.

Jenna: Do you have any errands for me ______(11)______? I'd be willing ______(12)______ at the store for you. I'd be happy ______(13)______ some groceries for dinner tonight.

Mother: I guess that would be all right. Now that I think about it, it will be pretty convenient for me ______(14)______ another licensed driver in the house!

12 Practice

Rewrite the sentences using infinitives instead of gerunds.

1. Obeying traffic laws is important.

   It's important to obey traffic laws.

2. Understanding how your car works is necessary.

   ____

3. Failing a driving test is disappointing.

   ____

4. Not having a car is frustrating for some teenagers.

   ____

5. Driving without insurance is illegal.

   ____

6. Not wearing a seatbelt is dangerous.

   ____

7. For young people, getting their driver's license is very exciting.

   ____

8. Owning and maintaining a car can be expensive.

   ____

9. Saving money for a car isn't easy for everyone.

   ____

9f *Too* and *Enough* Followed by Infinitives

Student Book p. 278

13 Practice

Jared likes his English class better than his psychology class. Use information from the chart to write three sentences about the classes using *too, enough,* and *not . . . enough*.

	Psychology Class	English Class
1	There are so many people that not everyone has a chair to sit on.	There are plenty of chairs for everyone to sit on.
2	The professor speaks so softly that the students in the back can't hear him.	The professor speaks loudly, and everyone can hear.
3	The professor speaks so quickly that Jared can't take notes.	The professor speaks slowly, and Jared can take notes.
4	The windows are so high that they can't be opened.	The windows are low, and they can be opened.
5	The class is at 8:00 A.M., and the students are so tired that they can't pay attention.	The class is at 10:00 A.M.; the students are awake and can pay attention.
6	The students are so lazy that they don't do the homework.	The students are so motivated that they always do the homework.

1. a. *In Jared's psychology class, there are too many people for everyone to have a chair.*

b. *In his psychology class, there aren't enough chairs for everyone to sit on.*

c. *In his English class, there are enough chairs for eveyone to sit on.*

2. a. The professor in his psychology class ______________________________

b. In his psychology class, ______________________________

c. In his English class, ______________________________

3. a. The psychology professor ______________________________

b. The psychology professor ______________________________

c. The English professor ______________________________

4. a. In the psychology classroom, ______________________________

b. In the psychology classroom, ______________________________

c. In the English classroom, ______________________________

5. a. In the 8:00 A.M. psychology class, ______________________________

b. In the 8:00 A.M. psychology class, ______________________________

c. In the 10:00 A.M. English class, ______________________________

6. a. The psychology students ______________________________

b. The psychology students ______________________________

c. The English students ______________________________

14 Practice

Complete the sentences with *too, enough, not . . . enough,* or *very.*

1. I can't afford to take a vacation. I don't have ________________ money.
2. There is ________________ time to review for the test, so we'll do that in class tomorrow.
3. We're ________________ tired, but we'll go to your party anyway.
4. I'm sorry we're ________________ tired to go to your party, but thanks for inviting us.
5. It's ________________ dangerous to ice skate on the pond — don't do it!
6. Are there ________________ people to get a group discount?
7. Roberta is ________________ smart; she got all A's last semester.
8. You should have the last piece of cake; there is ________________ for two people.
9. In the United States, eighteen is old ________________ to vote.
10. Some people think that fifteen-year-olds are ________________ young to date.

15 Practice

Write five sentences about the photograph. Use *too, enough,* and *not . . . enough* with infinitives.

1. ______________________________
2. ______________________________
3. ______________________________
4. ______________________________
5. ______________________________

9g Showing Purpose

Student Book p. 281

16 Practice

Rewrite each sentence twice, replacing *for* with the verbs in parentheses. The first time, use an infinitive. The second time, use the more formal *in order to* + a base verb.

1. David went to the library for a book about Spain. (locate)
   a. *David went to the library to locate a book about Spain.*
   b. *David went to the library in order to locate a book about Spain.*
2. David wanted to visit Spain for his relatives there. (see)
   a. ______________________________
   b. ______________________________
3. He studied the book for information about his family's town. (find)
   a. ______________________________
   b. ______________________________

4. He got a summer job for travel money. (earn)

a. ______________________________

b. ______________________________

5. He signed up at the community center for Spanish classes. (take)

a. ______________________________

b. ______________________________

6. He used the Internet for a cheap airplane ticket to Spain. (buy)

a. ______________________________

b. ______________________________

17 Practice

Ellen has moved into a new apartment. What does she need to buy or do? Where must she go to buy or do these things? Write six sentences using *to, for,* and *in order to.*

Example: *She must go to the furniture store to buy furniture.*

1. ______________________________
2. ______________________________
3. ______________________________
4. ______________________________
5. ______________________________
6. ______________________________

18 Practice

What should you do in order not to have problems in school? Rewrite the following sentences using *in order not to* + a verb.

1. You should sit near the front of the class so you won't miss anything the teacher says.

   You should sit near the front of the class in order not to miss anything the teacher says.

2. You should review your notes so you won't forget information.

   ____

3. You should buy file folders so you won't lose your papers.

   ____

4. You should allow plenty of time to get to class so you won't be late.

   ____

5. You should buy a day planner or a PDA so you won't waste time.

   ____

6. You should get enough sleep and exercise so you won't get sick.

   ____

7. You should join student clubs so you won't feel lonely.

   ____

8. You should ask your teachers for help so you won't fall behind.

   ____

9. (*your own advice*)

   ____

10. (*your own advice*)

   ____

9h Perfect Infinitives and Perfect Gerunds; Passive Voice of Infinitives and Gerunds

Student Book p. 283

19 Practice

Read why Jim was late for work. Complete the sentences using the perfect infinitive or perfect gerund form of the verbs in parentheses. Some sentences require the active voice (*to have* + past participle or *having* + past participle). Others require the passive voice (*to have been* + past participle or *having been* + past participle).

I had such a terrible morning! After (wake up) having woken up (1) an hour late, I couldn't find my car keys anywhere. Then I remembered that I had put them in my brown pants, which I had taken to be cleaned yesterday. (warn) ______ (2) not to come late to work again, I knew there was no time to waste. I ran down the street to the bus stop. I thought I was really smart (remember) ______ (3) the 8:30 bus. But I couldn't figure out why no one else was at the bus stop. Then I looked at the schedule. The schedule had changed, and the bus now came at 8:20. I was angry with myself for (not, look) ______ (4) at the schedule before (leave) ______ (5) my house. After (miss) ______ (6) the bus, I decided my only option was to run to work. Then, after (run) ______ (7) two miles to the office, I sat down at my desk. I wasn't happy (arrive) ______ (8) fifteen minutes late. But I thought I was really lucky (not, notice) ______ (9) by the boss. I expected (call) ______ (10) into his office before I even sat down. Then I heard that the boss, (take) ______ (11) the day off, isn't even here today!

20 Practice

Rewrite each sentence about the photo twice, using *need* + a gerund and *need* + a passive infinitive (*to be* + past participle). Use the verbs in parentheses.

1. There are too many papers on Barbara's desk. (file)

   a. The papers need filing.

   b. The papers need to be filed.

2. There are 28 voicemail messages on her phone. (delete)

   a. ______

   b. ______

3. Three meetings must be set up before 4:00. (schedule)

   a. ______

   b. ______

4. The computer is down. (service)

   a. ______

   b. ______

5. The copy machine is broken. (repair)

   a. ______

   b. ______

6. Her assistant quit this morning. (replace)

   a. ______

   b. ______

9i Base verbs + *-ing* with Verbs of Perception

Student Book p. 287

21 Practice

Read the following police report. Decide if the events describe a single complete action or an action in progress. If it is a single complete action, circle the base verb form. If it is an action in progress, circle the gerund form.

Police Report

At 6:00 P.M. in Shoreline Park, a 25-year-old woman named Ji Lee witnessed a crime. She was reading a book when she heard something (move / moving) in the bushes behind her. She turned around and saw a man in the process of (crawl / crawling)[1] towards an elderly woman who was sitting at a park bench. The older woman did not seem to notice the man (come / coming)[2] towards her. Ji watched the man (walk / walking)[3] to the end of the path and (stopping / stop)[4] just behind the woman's purse. She realized she was observing a crime (happen / happening)[5] before her eyes!

She didn't want the thief to turn around and see her (watch / watching)[6] him, so she moved behind a tree. Earlier, she had seen the man (put / putting)[7] his hand in his pocket as he approached the bench, and she thought he might have a weapon! She observed the man's hand (reach / reaching)[8] down into the woman's purse. Ji shouted, "Help!", but there was no one around to hear her (shout / shouting)[9]. Fortunately, she surprised the man. She watched the man quickly (remove / removing)[10] his hand from the woman's bag and then (run / running)[11] away. Having seen a crime (be / being)[12] committed in this park, Ji isn't eager to return to it anytime soon.[13]

9j Person + Gerund

Student Book p. 288

22 Practice

Rewrite the sentences with a person + a gerund. Give answers in both informal and formal English.

1. My friend Beth talks on her cell phone when we go out for coffee. I don't like it.
   a. *I don't like Beth talking on her cell phone when we go out for coffee.*
   b. *I don't like Beth's talking on her cell phone when we go out for coffee.*
2. Her friends call and interrupt our conversation. I can't stand it.
   a. ______
   b. ______
3. They don't ask her if she's free to talk on the phone. I don't approve of that.
   a. ______
   b. ______
4. My boyfriend turns his phone off in restaurants. I appreciate that.
   a. ______
   b. ______

5. He doesn't want to hear the phone ring in public places. I respect that.

a. ______________________________

b. ______________________________

6. On the other hand, sometimes my boyfriend doesn't answer the phone when I call. I'm annoyed by that.

a. ______________________________

b. ______________________________

7. Beth ignores me when her friends call. I'm tired of it.

a. ______________________________

b. ______________________________

8. I politely ask her to get off the phone. She doesn't hear me.

a. ______________________________

b. ______________________________

23 Practice

Read the sentences. Write *C* next to the sentence if the "person + gerund" pattern is used correctly. Write *I* if it is used incorrectly.

_____ **1.** My sister and I have never been close, so I was surprised at asking me to be the maid of honor in her wedding.

_____ **2.** Chris loves to listen to the symphony. He especially enjoys they playing free concerts in the park.

_____ **3.** Janet was tired of her friends' criticizing her clothing style.

_____ **4.** Rick's parents didn't hear his getting in late.

_____ **5.** The instructor couldn't stand the students talking in class.

_____ **6.** Her friends laugh at her singing.

_____ **7.** We were encouraged by the governor supports education.

_____ **8.** Do you mind them clean the house while you are working?

SELF-TEST

A Choose the best answer, A, B, C, or D, to complete the sentence. Mark your answer by darkening the oval with the same letter.

1. I don't remember ____________ to Europe when I was two years old.

A. to go (A) (B) (C) (D)
B. going
C. for to go
D. for going

2. The new employee isn't capable ____________ doing the job.

A. in (A) (B) (C) (D)
B. to
C. of
D. about

3. Some people cut up their credit cards in order ____________ them.

A. not to use (A) (B) (C) (D)
B. for not to use
C. to use
D. not use

4. The teacher is always willing ____________ students with their assignments.

A. for to help (A) (B) (C) (D)
B. helping
C. help
D. to help

5. The coach didn't ____________ five games in a row.

A. expect us win (A) (B) (C) (D)
B. expect to us win
C. expect win
D. expect us to win

6. Stella wanted ____________ the assignment by lunchtime because she expected ____________ to present her work to the class that afternoon.

A. to have been finished / being asked (A) (B) (C) (D)
B. to have finished / to be asked
C. to have been finishing / to be asked
D. to finish / having been asked

7. I was pleased at ____________ good grades.

A. to have earned (A) (B) (C) (D)
B. having earned
C. earning
D. had earned

8. We regret ____________ you that we cannot offer you the job at this time.

A. to inform (A) (B) (C) (D)
B. informing
C. for informing
D. informed

9. Francie resented ____________ to the event at the last minute.

A. to have been invited (A) (B) (C) (D)
B. having invited
C. having been invited
D. to have invited

10. The girls are ____________ to go to the rock concert alone; it's not safe.

A. too young (A) (B) (C) (D)
B. young enough
C. not young enough
D. young

B **Find the underlined word or phrase, A, B, C, or D, that is incorrect. Mark your answer by darkening the oval with the same letter.**

1. I used to enjoy going (A) running (B), but I stopped to run (C) after I injured (D) my knee.

Ⓐ Ⓑ Ⓒ Ⓓ

2. What would stop (A) the world champion for (B) winning (C) the Boston Marathon next week (D)?

Ⓐ Ⓑ Ⓒ Ⓓ

3. When Emily refused (A) to clean her room (B), her parents wouldn't (C) allow to watch (D) TV.

Ⓐ Ⓑ Ⓒ Ⓓ

4. If you have some time (A) for to discuss (B) the proposal, I'm eager to talk (C) about it with you (D).

Ⓐ Ⓑ Ⓒ Ⓓ

5. He doesn't need (A) making (B) a lot of money, but he would like (C) to have (D) a fun job.

Ⓐ Ⓑ Ⓒ Ⓓ

6. If you're taking (A) a long trip, don't forget (B) checking (C) the oil in your car before you go (D).

Ⓐ Ⓑ Ⓒ Ⓓ

7. My sister was (A) thrilled to have been (B) chose (C) to represent (D) the company at the conference last season.

Ⓐ Ⓑ Ⓒ Ⓓ

8. For to purchase (A) this ticket, it's necessary (B) to show (C) your identification (D) at the counter.

Ⓐ Ⓑ Ⓒ Ⓓ

9. The family was happy (A) to have (B) found (C) their lost dog after searched (D) for many weeks.

Ⓐ Ⓑ Ⓒ Ⓓ

10. Having argued (A) with the neighbors, I was surprised (B) at they (C) bringing (D) us a nice gift.

Ⓐ Ⓑ Ⓒ Ⓓ

UNIT 10 AGREEMENT AND PARALLEL STRUCTURE

10a Subject-Verb Agreement: General Rules Part 1

Student Book p. 302

1 Practice

Complete the sentences by circling the correct form of the verbs in parentheses.

Sports Unlimited Fitness Center

April Newsletter

Greetings, members! This month we would like to inform you about new classes and facilities at our gym. You will find that many changes (has / **have**) [1] been made.

First of all, the new building (is / are) [2] finished. This news (is / are) [3] good for tennis players: the building (contain / contains) [4] two tennis courts! Playing basketball (is / are) [5] also something that members can enjoy in the new building. Two courts (has / have) [6] been built in the back of this building.

The women's locker room (has / have) [7] been moved to the new building as well. New showers, a Jacuzzi, and a sauna (were / was) [8] installed there last week. The men's lockers and sauna (is / are) [9] still located in the old building. However, plans to remodel the men's locker room next year (is / are) [10] currently being discussed.

All members (is / are) [11] required to get a new ID card. Electronics (is / are) [12] changing our ID card system. Scanning a bar code (replace / replaces) [13] the old paper card system. Susan and Joe (has / have) [14] the new plastic cards for you at the front desk. Until the end of this month, either the old cards or the new cards (work / works) [15]. After this month, however, all the old cards (stop / stops) [16] working.

Step aerobics (is / are) [17] now a class offered at our gym! Step classes (is / are) [18] held Monday through Friday at 6:00 A.M. and 6:00 P.M. Tuesday and Thursday (is / are) [19] the most popular days for these classes, so be sure to sign up in advance. If you're looking for a spinning class, Monday morning or Wednesday evening (is / are) the best time to go. If you've never tried spinning, all of our instructors (is / are) happy to schedule a thirty-minute private lesson and (show / shows) you how to use the bike.

20 21 22

2 Practice

Think of a group such as a class, a school, a gym, a sports team, or a club. Write sentences about this group. Explain what people do or have to do. Use the simple present or the present perfect and the quantity words.

Example: *I belong to a chorus. All members come to practice every day at 4:00.*
Most people in the group have been singing for a long time.
Everyone loves to perform at the concerts. Not everyone has taken private singing lessons. . .

1. All ______________________________.
2. Most ______________________________.
3. Some ______________________________.
4. Each ______________________________.
5. Every ______________________________.
6. Everyone ______________________________.
7. Not everyone ______________________________.
8. Any ______________________________.
9. Almost all ______________________________.

10b Subject-Verb Agreement: General Rules Part 2

Student Book p. 305

3 Practice

Complete the sentences with a singular or plural form of *be*. Pay attention to time words; use present and past tenses when necessary.

There ____*is*____ (1) good news for our soccer team these days. Yesterday's game, despite concerns about the weather, ________ (2) a major victory: the Cobras ________ (3) now headed to the community league playoffs!

Co-captain Dennis Garcia, along with Co-captain Beth Carlson, ________ (4) very excited about this next step. Garcia explains, "Going to the playoffs, which will take place next week, ________ (5) the highest honor this team could hope for. We've faced a lot of challenges this season. But those lost games, together with the lost hopes, ________ (6) now far behind us. We ________ (7) a championship team!"

Carlson adds, "Bad weather, as well as the loss of some players, ________ (8) something that every team has to face at some point. But there were a lot of concerns back in the beginning of the season. There ________ (9) many new players who joined our team, and there ________ (10) more injured players than we've had in the past. There ________ (11) also a new coach who joined our team halfway through the season. Whenever a team goes through that amount of change, there ________ (12) always going to be some confusion. There ________ (13) certainly going to be lost matches and lost hopes while the team works to redefine itself."

Rich Regan, the new coach, ______ (14) perhaps more excited than any of his players. "The Cobras, even with this year's losses, ______ (15) showing great improvement from previous years," says Coach Regan. "And the great thing about my coming into the season halfway through ______ (16) the chance to bring in new energy and fresh hopes."

This year the Cobras, minus the five players who have left the team, ______ (17) fighting back with their new coach and new, talented players. Regan, Garcia, and Carlson ______ (18) all optimistic that the chances of winning the playoffs ______ (19) very high. The group of new players ______ (20) beginning to show great talent. One of the new players, Isabella Cherrez, ______ (21) especially worth watching, according to Coach Regan.

Unfortunately, rain, along with high winds, ______ (22) predicted for Saturday's match. But the players, together with their captains and coach, ______ (23) not likely to have their spirits dampened. This ______ (24) a team with a winning spirit, and there ______ (25) no doubt that they will fight hard to win this important match.

4 Practice

Describe the photographs. Complete the sentences with your own ideas. Use *be* or other verbs in the simple present or present progressive. Make sure that subjects and verbs agree.

A.

1. All of these people *are trying to fit into the doorway.*

2. One of these people ______________________________

3. All of these people ______________________________

4. Almost all of these people ______________________________

5. Half of these people ______________________________

B.

1. All four of these boys ______________________________

____

2. Two of the boys ______________________________

____

3. The small boy in the striped shirt ______________________________

____

4. One of the older boys ______________________________

____

5. The challenge for three of the boys ______________________________

____

C.

1. The little girl together with her parents

____

____

2. Everyone in this family ______________________________

____

3. The parents of the little girl ______________________________

4. The exciting thing for her parents ______________________________

10c Subject-Verb Agreement with Quantity Words

Student Book p. 307

5 Practice

Complete the sentences with the correct form of the verbs in parentheses. Note that these sentences talk about people, not time, money, distance, or weight.

1. Some of the facts about this year's graduating class (be) ____are____ fascinating.
2. Two-thirds of the graduating seniors (plan) ______________ to attend a four-year college or a community college.

3. Almost half of them (want) ____________________ to attend graduate school someday.
4. Over half of the seniors (have) ____________________ been accepted into a four-year college for the fall.
5. Most of our school's graduates (attend) ____________________ the state university.
6. The number of students accepted into the state university (increase) ____________________ every year.
7. A number of seniors (work) ____________________ part-time while attending school.
8. Some of the students (have) ____________________ job offers already.
9. Five percent of the graduating class (have) ____________________ won national honors.
10. One of the seniors (be) ____________________ the recipient of a four-year scholarship to Yale University.
11. Some of the graduation ceremony (be) ____________________ reserved to honor award-winning students.
12. Every one of the students (make) ____________________ his or her teacher proud!
13. None of the students (miss) ____________________ graduation day.
14. Four years (be) ____________________ a long time to work on earning a diploma.

6 Practice

Read the sentences. Write *C* next to the sentence if the subject and verb used with the quantity word agree and the sentence is correct. Write *I* if they do not agree and the sentence is incorrect.

_____ **1.** Five minutes is all the time I have to speak with you.

_____ **2.** Some of the flowers has died.

_____ **3.** A number of people suffers from migraine headaches.

_____ **4.** None of the critics likes the new movie.

_____ **5.** Five hours are not enough sleep for most people.

_____ **6.** You can borrow any of my books, but some of them belong to the library.

_____ **7.** One of the lamps in the living room are broken.

_____ **8.** Our state is very dry this summer, and two inches of rain aren't going to be enough to solve the problem.

_____ **9.** Two-thirds of people under twenty-five do not have health insurance.

_____ **10.** The number of crimes committed last year are frightening.

10d Parallel Structure

Student Book p. 311

7 Practice

Underline the parallel structure in the following sentences. Then write which grammatical form (nouns, adjectives, verbs, adverbs, gerunds, or infinitives) the parallel structures contain.

1. Domino tiles are <u>thick</u> and <u>heavy</u> enough to stand on edge. *adjectives*

2. Dominoes is a very popular game in South America, Asia, and North America. _____________

3. Learning how to play dominoes is easy, but winning dominoes requires strategy. _____________

4. If you look at a domino with many dots and a domino with fewer dots, the "heavier" domino is the one with more dots. _____________

5. To begin playing dominoes, place the tiles face down on a table and shuffle them by hand. _____________

6. Players take turns placing tiles on the table, matching the number of dots to those already laid down, and decreasing their amount of tiles. ______________

7. The object of the game might be to play all of one's tiles, or to have the highest score at the end of the game. ______________

8. There are two main types of domino games: block games and draw games. ______________

9. In a block game, if players can't play and eliminate any of their tiles, they lose their turn. ______________

10. In a draw game, players take new tiles from the common pile and don't stop until they get one they can play. ______________

11. Dominoes is an exciting and strategic game that can be enjoyed by people of all ages. ______________

12. Many serious dominoes players compete in regional, national, and international tournaments. ______________

8 Practice

Correct the errors in parallel structure. Then write which grammatical form (nouns, adjectives, verbs, adverbs, gerunds, or infinitives) the parallel structures contain. Some sentences have no errors.

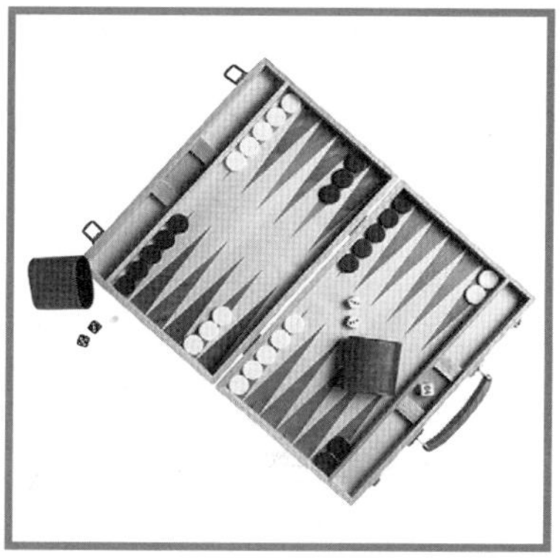

1. Backgammon, a game for two players, requires a backgammon set, two sets of dice, and ~~you need~~ thirty checkers. ______nouns______

2. The backgammon board has twenty-four triangles, which lie in four quadrants and alternating in color. ______________

3. A bar down the center of the board separates the players' "home board" and "outer board." ______________

4. The objects of the game are to move all of your checkers around the board, to bring them to your own home board, and taking them off the board. ______________

5. The first player to move all of his or her checkers and to take them off the board wins the game. ____________

6. Players must roll the dice again if a die fallen outside the board, hits a checker, or does not land flat. ____________

7. If a player's move is unfinished or illegality, the opponent is allowed to accept that move. ____________

9 Practice

Answer the following questions with information about yourself. Use parallel structure and correct punctuation.

1. What are (or were) your three favorite subjects in school?

   My favorite subjects in school are chemistry, math, and art.

2. What three adjectives best describe you?

   ____

3. What are two things that you do every morning?

   ____

4. What three chores around the house do you dislike doing?

   ____

5. What are three things that you want to do in the future?

   ____

6. What are two things that you don't want to do in the future?

   ____

7. In your opinion, what three activities are the most useful for relieving stress?

   ____

8. In your opinion, what are the two biggest causes of stress among people your age?

   ____

9. What are two words that describe how you speak English?

   ____

10. What are three things that someone should do or see if they visit your city?

   ____

10 Practice

Write a paragraph about a game that you know. Explain what materials you need and how to play the game. Check your sentences for parallel structure and correct punctuation.

____

____

____

____

____

____

____

10e Coordinating Conjunctions

Student Book p. 314

11 Practice

Combine each pair of sentences into one longer sentence using a coordinating conjunction. Use correct punctuation.

1. Alicia wants to buy fruit. She doesn't know what kind.

   Alicia wants to buy fruit,

   but she doesn't know what kind.

2. The grapefruit looks ripe. The plums look very fresh.

   ____

   ____

3. Apples are on sale today. She should buy a lot of them.

   ____

   ____

4. She could use fresh fruit in a dessert. She could use it in a salad instead.

   ____

5. The strawberries look delicious. They are too expensive.

   ____

6. She should shop at the farmer's market. The prices are lower. The fruit is fresher.

____

7. Alicia would like to make an apple pie. She doesn't know how.

____

8. If she wants to bake a pie, she should buy a baking dish. She doesn't have one.

____

12 Practice

Write a paragraph of at least six sentences describing this house. Use each coordinating conjunction (*and, for, or, so, but, yet*) at least once. Use correct punctuation.

____

____

____

____

____

____

13 Practice

Read the sentences for errors with conjunctions or with commas. If the sentence is correct, write *C*. If the sentence is incorrect, write *I* and correct the error(s).

_____ **1.** My sister was always good at math, so I was always better at English.

_____ **2.** Jacob applied for six jobs, for he didn't get any of them.

_____ **3.** We were very tired, but we stayed up and studied anyway.

_____ **4.** The actor was seventy years old yet he was still very handsome.

_____ **5.** You can leave a voicemail message or you can call back later.

_____ **6.** They tried to take notes, and they couldn't hear the teacher.

_____ **7.** Drew's parents are coming to visit, and they are bringing lots of food for him.

_____ **8.** The movie was so bad that we wanted to leave, or we stayed and watched until the end.

10f Correlative Conjunctions: *Both . . . And; Not Only . . . But Also; Either . . . Or; Neither . . . Nor*

Student Book p. 317

14 Practice

Read the sentences about twin brothers. Circle the correct form of the verbs in parentheses.

1. Both Brandon and Roger (is / are) seniors at Garfield High School.
2. Both Brandon and his brother (plan / plans) to attend college.
3. Neither the twins nor their parents (want / wants) a college that is far from home.
4. Both Brandon and Roger (prefers/ prefer) to go to the same college.
5. Either the University of Michigan or Michigan State (are / is) a good choice for the brothers.
6. Not only Roger's teachers but also Roger (think / thinks) that Michigan State will accept him.
7. Either business or economics (interest / interests) Brandon.
8. Neither mathematics nor political science (interest / interests) Roger.
9. Not only the University of Michigan but also Michigan State (offer / offers) basketball scholarships.
10. Either a grant or student loans (is / are) going to be useful for paying for college, since both boys will be studying at the same time.

15 Practice

Combine each pair of sentences into one longer sentence. Use the correlative conjunctions in parentheses.

1. Roger plays basketball. Brandon plays basketball. (both / and)

   Both Roger and Brandon play basketball.

2. Roger plays basketball. Brandon plays basketball. (not only / but also)

   ____

3. Roger does not like math. Brandon does not like math. (neither / nor)

   ____

4. Roger does not enjoy math. He does not enjoy history. (neither / nor)

   ____

5. Roger does not enjoy math. He does not enjoy history. (either / or)

   ____

6. Brandon works on the weekends or he goes out with his friends. (either / or)

   ____

7. Brandon likes fixing cars or repairing electronic equipment for fun. (either / or)

   ____

8. The twins like spending time with each other. Their parents like spending time with each other. (both / and)

   ____

   ____

9. Roger's mother wants the boys to choose a college close to home. Roger's father wants the boys to choose a college close to home. (not only / but also)

   ____

   ____

10. Roger's mother wants the boys to visit often. She wants her sons to be independent. (not only / but also)

    ____

    ____

16 Practice

Write sentences about each pair of jobs. Use correlative conjunctions and your own ideas.

Example: *Both veterinarians and medical doctors need to study medicine. Not only medical doctors but also veterinarians want to help others get well.*

A.

Veterinarian (Vet)

Medical Doctor

1. both / and

____

2. not only / but also

____

3. neither / nor

____

4. either / or

____

B.

Chef

Waiter

1. both / and

____

2. not only / but also

____

3. neither / nor

____

4. either / or

____

C. Think of two other jobs and compare them using correlative conjunctions in your own sentences.

Job 1: ______________ Job 2: ______________

1. both / and

____

2. not only / but also

____

3. neither / nor

____

4. either / or

____

SELF-TEST

A Choose the best answer, A, B, C, or D, to complete the sentence. Mark your answer by darkening the oval with the same letter.

1. I've always enjoyed seeing my family and _______.

A. to talk about old times (A) (B) (C) (D)
B. talking about old times
C. talked about old times
D. talk about old times

2. My friend hopes to attend either _______ next fall.

A. Seattle University or Pacific University (A) (B) (C) (D)
B. Seattle University nor Pacific University
C. Seattle University and Pacific University
D. to Seattle University and to Pacific University

3. The instructor never arrived, _______ the students went home.

A. but (A) (B) (C) (D)
B. so
C. or
D. for

4. Jane's mother will _______.

A. buy her neither a car nor lend her one (A) (B) (C) (D)
B. not neither buy her a car nor lend her one
C. buy her a car nor lend her one
D. neither buy her a car nor lend her one

5. Neither Greg _______ happy with the test results.

A. or his teachers are (A) (B) (C) (D)
B. or his teachers is
C. nor his teachers are
D. nor his teachers is

6. The doctor told him to exercise, _______ he didn't take the doctor's advice.

A. but (A) (B) (C) (D)
B. for
C. or
D. so

7. Many people dislike New England's summers because of the _______.

A. hot and humidity (A) (B) (C) (D)
B. heat and humidity
C. heat and humid
D. hot and humid

8. The car makes not only a loud noise _______.

A. but a bad smell also (A) (B) (C) (D)
B. also a bad smell
C. but also a bad smell
D. but also makes a bad smell

9. If you feel _______, you should call a doctor.

A. pain, tired, and thirsty (A) (B) (C) (D)
B. pain, tired, and thirst
C. pain, tiredness, and thirsty
D. pain, tiredness, and thirst

10. The computer _______.

A. both has a flat screen and new speakers (A) (B) (C) (D)
B. both have a flat screen and new speakers
C. has both a flat screen and new speakers
D. a flat screen and new speakers both

B Find the underlined word or phrase, A, B, C, or D, that is incorrect. Mark your answer by darkening the oval with the same letter.

1. Thirty minutes are (A) not enough time (B) for some students to take (C) the test and to do well (D).

   (A) (B) (C) (D)

2. The instructions (A) for building the (B) patio table is (C) difficult to understand (D).

   (A) (B) (C) (D)

3. Each (A) of the presidential candidates promise (B) to lower taxes (C) and to spend (D) more money on education.

   (A) (B) (C) (D)

4. Economics don't (A) usually interest me, (B) but (C) my economics class is (D) really exciting.

   (A) (B) (C) (D)

5. There is (A) many reasons why mathematics is useful (B) not only in school but also (C) for work (D).

   (A) (B) (C) (D)

6. The number of (A) traffic accidents caused by (B) cell phones are (C) increasing (D) every year.

   (A) (B) (C) (D)

7. Falling in love (A) can make people feel (B) happiness (C), tired, and worried (D) all at once.

   (A) (B) (C) (D)

8. There is (A) a lot of traffic (B) at this time of day, for (C) we should wait an hour until the roads are (D) less busy.

   (A) (B) (C) (D)

9. Either the ocean or (A) the mountains is (B) a good place to go for (C) a vacation, but (D) the choice is yours.

   (A) (B) (C) (D)

10. Ed was feeling tired all the time, so (A) the doctor recommended both (B) exercising more (C) and to take (D) vitamins.

   (A) (B) (C) (D)

UNIT 11 NOUN CLAUSES AND REPORTED SPEECH

11a Noun Clauses Beginning with *That*

Student Book p. 328

1 Practice

Read the sentences. Write *C* next to the sentence if the *that* noun clause is correct. Write *I* if it is incorrect.

_____ **1.** That you don't know what you're doing is clear.

_____ **2.** We believe your work is not up to standard.

_____ **3.** I don't hope so.

_____ **4.** I hope not.

_____ **5.** He's a manager doesn't change things.

_____ **6.** They think so.

_____ **7.** We think so.

_____ **8.** You thought so that he was here.

_____ **9.** It's not surprising that he was fired.

_____ **10.** We can't prove not that the intern stole the money.

2 Practice

Read about Christopher Columbus. Underline the noun clauses. Some begin with *that* and others have *that* omitted.

Christopher Columbus, originally from Genoa, Italy, was an explorer who knew the world was round. He predicted he could find a trade route to Asia by sailing west. He had a very difficult time raising money for his voyage, so he finally appealed to Queen Isabella and King Ferdinand of Spain. They decided that Columbus might be right, and it would be in the best interest of Spain to find out. Columbus set out to prove that he was right.

On his first voyage in 1492, he arrived in the Bahamas and established a settlement there, but he thought he had arrived in Asia, and when he went back to Spain, he told the king and queen that he had. Many people doubted that this was true. On his second trip, Columbus discovered his original settlement had been destroyed, and he had to spend most of his time governing instead of exploring. He was an unfit governor, and although he made a total of four trips to the New World, he died regretting he had never found the route to Asia that he was convinced existed.

3 Practice

Write negative responses using the verbs in parentheses and *so* or *not*.

1. Boss: Can you stay late tonight?

Kevin: I (be afraid) _'m afraid not_. My wife is working tonight, so I have to pick up the kids.

2. Kevin: Sean, are you working late tonight?

Sean: I (hope) ___________.

3. Sean: Do you have any printer paper?

Jackie: I (think) ___________, but I'll look.

4. Jackie: Are you leaving now? It's 5:00.

Sean: I (guess) ___________ because I have to finish this before tomorrow.

5. Sean: Do you have a little money I could borrow? I'll pay you back tomorrow.

Jackie: I (believe) ___________. I went shopping at lunch, and I think I spent all my cash.

Now respond to the following statements using *think, believe, be afraid, guess,* or *hope.* Use *so* or *not* where appropriate. Explain your answer.

6. The polar ice caps will stop melting.

____.

7. Women will receive the same salary as men in the next ten years.

____.

8. The spread of AIDS in Africa will stop.

____.

9. Movie theaters will disappear.

____.

10. Everyone should have cosmetic surgery if they want it.

____.

4 Practice

Read about Matt and his family. Then complete the sentences using the prompts.

My brother, Matt, his wife, and his son used to live in the Virgin Islands. In the late summer and fall, the island they lived on was threatened by hurricanes. One year, they knew that a hurricane was coming, so they made as many preparations as possible and sat back and waited for it to come. Late in the night, Matt was woken up when his cat, Sasha, stood on his chest and meowed very loudly in Matt's ear. Finally, Matt woke up and knew something was wrong. The sound of rain was different—louder. Matt got up and went up to check the attic. What he saw shocked him. Most of the roof had been torn away by the wind. As he stood there, more of the roof disappeared into the sky. Matt knew that if they stayed, the house would collapse on top of them. Matt quickly woke up the family, grabbed Sasha, and went to a neighbor's house. The next day, they looked at what was left of their home. If Sasha hadn't woken Matt up, his family could have been seriously injured.

1. Matt thought *that he'd made his house safe*.

2. Sasha knew ____.

3. Matt discovered ____.

4. He observed ____.

5. He realized ____.

6. He decided ____.

7. Matt and his family believe ______________________________________.

5 Practice

Complete the sentences.

1. Nostradamus predicted (that) ____________________________________.
2. Ancient Egyptians believed (that) ________________________________.
3. Galileo observed (that) ____.
4. Sigmund Freud thought (that) ____________________________________.
5. Hackers show (that) ____.
6. Actors dream (that) ____.
7. Babies learn (that) ____.
8. Everyone knows (that) ____.
9. As I've grown older, I've noticed (that) ___________________________.
10. The people of my country think (that) ____________________________.

11b Noun Clauses Beginning with Wh- Words (Indirect Wh- Questions)

Student Book p. 331

6 Practice

Read the sentences. Write *C* next to the sentence if the noun clause beginning with a wh- word (indirect wh- question) is correct. Write *I* if it is incorrect.

_____ 1. Do you know where is Kevin?

_____ 2. Do you know where Kevin is?

_____ 3. I don't know what is his name.

_____ 4. I don't know what his name is.

_____ 5. We're not sure what he does for a living.

_____ **6.** We're not sure what does he do for a living.

_____ **7.** Could you tell me where is the restroom?

_____ **8.** Could you tell me where the restroom is?

_____ **9.** Her parents wanted to know what her plans are.

_____ **10.** Her parents wanted to know what are her plans.

_____ **11.** Did you hear what did she say?

_____ **12.** Did you hear what she said?

7 Practice

Before you get a pet, you should ask yourself questions to be sure that you can care for your new family member. Write indirect wh- questions using "I know."

1. How should I take care of him?

I know how I should take care of him.

2. What does he eat?

____.

3. When does he sleep?

____.

4. What kind of toys does he like?

____.

5. When should I take him to the vet?

____.

6. What other equipment do I need?

____.

7. When should I feed him?

____.

8. How long will he live?

____.

9. What else should I know?

____.

8 Practice

Write direct questions from the indirect wh- questions.

1. I didn't hear what she said.

   What did she say?

2. I'm not sure when we're supposed to be there.

   ______________________________?

3. She didn't tell me what we should bring.

   ______________________________?

4. Did she tell you when the party starts?

   ______________________________?

5. Do you know who she invited?

   ______________________________?

6. Do you know where she lives?

   ______________________________?

7. Does anyone know how we can get there from here?

   ______________________________?

9 Practice

Read the situations. Write indirect wh- questions using the hints or your own ideas.

A. Your son just got engaged to a woman you don't know. Write indirect questions about her starting with "Your mother/father and I would like to know ...."

education	job
family	time for us to meet her
hometown	where you met

1. Your mother/father and I would like to know where you met her.
2. ______________________________.
3. ______________________________.
4. ______________________________.
5. ______________________________.
6. ______________________________.

B. You're on a tour, but you signed up at the last minute and have a lot of questions for the tour operator. Write indirect questions with "Could you tell me...."

activities	local architecture
cities to visit	meal times
historical sites	shopping opportunities

1. Could you tell me *where we'll be able to do a little shopping?*
2. ______________________________?
3. ______________________________?
4. ______________________________?
5. ______________________________?
6. ______________________________?

C. Your office is relocating. Ask your boss these indirect questions with "Do you know...." and your own ideas.

how long	where
what	why
when	

1. Do you know *what we should do with our files during the move?*
2. ______________________________?
3. ______________________________?
4. ______________________________?
5. ______________________________?
6. ______________________________?

D. A police officer is interviewing a suspect in a robbery case that happened last night at 9:00. Write indirect questions with "Tell us..." and your own ideas.

how	where
what	who with

1. Tell us *where you were last night at 9:00.*
2. ______________________________.
3. ______________________________.
4. ______________________________.
5. ______________________________.

11c Noun Clauses Beginning with *If* or *Whether* (Indirect Yes/No Questions)

Student Book p. 334

10 Practice

Read the sentences. Write *C* next to the sentence if the *if* or *whether* noun clause (indirect yes/no question) is correct. Write *I* if it is incorrect.

_____ **1.** I asked him if he takes the same bus every day.

_____ **2.** I asked him does he take the same bus every day.

_____ **3.** My cousin wanted to know if or not you could come, too.

_____ **4.** My cousin wanted to know whether or not you could come, too.

_____ **5.** She wants to know can she borrow the car.

_____ **6.** She wants to know if she can borrow the car.

_____ **7.** The authorities didn't say if they found the missing woman.

_____ **8.** The authorities didn't say whether they found the missing woman.

11 Practice

You want to plant a garden, and so you want to get information from people at the nursery. Write indirect questions using *if* or *whether* and "Could you tell me," "Do you know," or "I want to know."

1. Does this plant need a lot of light?

I want to know if this plant needs a lot of light.

2. Should I water these plants every day?

____

3. Do I need to prune these plants often?

____

4. Do I plant these in the spring or fall?

____

5. Will they grow in containers?

____

6. Will they attract butterflies?

____

7. Do these plants need a lot of care?

____

8. Should I fertilize them every week?

____

9. Will they come back next year?

____

12 Practice

Write direct questions from the indirect yes/no questions.

Marianne lives with two roommates, Sheryl and Kathy. Kathy is in Hawaii on vacation, and Sheryl is talking to her on the phone. Marianne is asking questions for Sheryl to ask Kathy.

1. Marianne: *Is she having a good time?*
   Sheryl: Marianne wants to know if you're having a good time.
2. Marianne: ____?
   Sheryl: Now she wants to know if you've met any cute guys.
3. Marianne: ____?
   Sheryl: Marianne has just asked me whether or not you've been to Waikiki yet.
4. Marianne: ____?
   Sheryl: Now she's just asked me if you're coming back soon.
5. Marianne: ____?
   Sheryl: She's wondering if you've tried surfing or not.
6. Marianne: ____?
   Sheryl: Now she wants to know if you've bought us any souvenirs.

13 Practice

Complete the indirect yes/no questions with your own ideas.

1. I've often wondered if I ______________________________.

2. I recently asked myself whether I ______________________________.

3. I'm not sure if I could ______________________________ or not.

4. I can't remember if I ______________________________ or not.

5. I don't know if ______________________________.

11d Quoted Speech

Student Book p. 337

14 Practice

Read the conversation between Lisa and Karl. Write *Q* next to the sentence if the statement is quoted speech. Write *R* if it is reported speech.

_____ **1.** "What's the weather like there?" Lisa asked.

_____ **2.** Karl told her it was foggy and windy.

_____ **3.** "I'm coming into the city tonight to see a play," she said.

_____ **4.** Karl said, "That sounds like fun."

_____ **5.** Lisa told Karl that the play had gotten very good reviews.

_____ **6.** Lisa said, "I got the tickets for my birthday."

_____ **7.** Karl told her to have a good time.

_____ **8.** Lisa said, "Thanks. Bye."

15 Practice

Insert quotation marks and correct punctuation in the phone conversation.

Hotel clerk: Hello

Todd: Hello. I was wondering if you have a vacancy for this weekend

Hotel clerk: Yes, we do

Todd: Great. Could we get a room with a queen size bed

Hotel clerk: Sorry. The only rooms left are ones with two double beds Will that work

Todd: That's fine

Hotel clerk:	Could I have your credit card number to hold the room
Todd:	Here you are. It's 333 2121 4646 0000
Hotel clerk:	Thank you sir. We'll see you this weekend

16 Practice

Match the quotation with the famous person who said it. Then write sentences in quoted speech using correct punctuation. Try to put *said* in different positions.

_____ **1.** Most folks are as happy as they make up their minds to be.

_____ **2.** I think, therefore, I am.

_____ **3.** Everyone will be famous for 15 minutes.

_____ **4.** Give a man a fish and you feed him for a day. Teach him how to fish and you feed him for a lifetime.

_____ **5.** A journey of a thousand miles begins with a single step.

a. Andy Warhol

b. Lao Tzu

c. Confucius

d. Rene Descartes

e. Abraham Lincoln

1. ____

____.

2. ____

____.

3. ____

____.

4. ____

____.

5. ____

____.

17 Practice

What are some things your parents and friends always say? Use correct punctuation.

1. My grandfather always said, *"If you lie down with dogs, you'll get up with fleas."*
2. My dad always says, ______
3. My mom always says, ______
4. My brother/sister says, ______
5. My best friend always says, ______

11e Reported Speech: Statements

Student Book p. 339

18 Practice

Read the sentences. Write *Q* next to the sentence if the statement is quoted speech. Write *R* if it is reported speech.

______ 1. "The new train schedule starts tomorrow," said Kim.

______ 2. The paper said the train schedule started the next day.

______ 3. It also said there would be fewer parking spaces at the station.

______ 4. The reporter said, "There will be fewer parking spaces."

______ 5. "Ticket prices are going up," said my neighbor.

______ 6. My neighbor told me that ticket prices were going up.

______ 7. The paper stated that routes would be cut.

______ 8. Mr. Rankin said, "Routes will be cut."

______ 9. I heard that the old station was being torn down.

______ 10. My bus driver said, "The old station is being torn down."

19 Practice

James Smith, a wealthy man who is not well liked, has disappeared. The police question his girlfriend, son, butler, and ex-wife. When the police officers report the interviews, change the quoted speech into reported speech.

1. His girlfriend said, "I hate him! He ruined my life. I wish he were dead."

   His girlfriend told us that she hated James Smith and that he had ruined her life. She told us that she wished he were dead.

2. His son said, "Father? I don't have a father. He left my sister and me when we were young and only came around once or twice a year. I hope he stays missing."

____

____.

3. His ex-wife said, "I haven't seen James since our divorce became final many years ago. I don't know where he is or what he's doing, and I don't care." ____________

____

____.

4. His butler said, "I'm not sure what his plans were yesterday. He is a very private man, and he rarely confides in me. He left the house around 9:00 in the morning yesterday, and he hasn't returned. That's why I called you." ____________

____

____.

20 Practice

Read the following situations. Then rewrite the quoted speech as reported speech.

1. Yesterday, Stephanie told her officemate, Kurt, about her vacation plans.

   "Last year we spent our vacation in Thailand. We thought about going back this year, but we decided to go camping instead. We're not leaving today. We're probably going to leave early tomorrow."

   Later, Kurt is telling another officemate about the conversation:

   Stephanie told me *that the year before they had spent their vacation*

   in Thailand.

   ____

   ____

2. Last night's news announcer said, "Millions of gallons of water have flooded farms near Highway 4 this morning. A levee gave way, and engineers have been studying the problem to determine the cause for the collapse. Workers have been working nonstop since this morning. We're going to join our correspondent who is live at the scene."

   Did you hear the news last night? The announcer said ____________

   ____

   ____

   ____

3. Tiffany, a 16-year-old high school student, is having a conversation with another girl from school on the subway home.

Melanie: I saw you talking with Chad.

Tiffany: I was not talking with Chad. He was talking with me.

Melanie: Well, he's my boyfriend, and I want you to stay away from him.

Tiffany: As if I'm interested! I was just giving him the English homework assignment. You need to get a life!

Later that night, Tiffany is talking to her friend Julie about the conversation:

Melanie said that she ____

____

____

____

____

____

4. Doug is telling his roommate about some family problems:

"I have to drop out of school because my parents' business isn't doing very well. I need to get a job and help them. I'll finish the semester, and then I'm going to move back home. I wish I could continue studying, but I can't."

Doug's roommate is telling his girlfriend about Doug's situation:

Doug said that he ____

____

____

____

____

____

21 Practice

Read the reported statements. Rewrite them as quoted speech.

A. Bob is explaining why he had to cancel his annual cookout this year:

The Andersons told me they couldn't come because one of their children was sick. Ms. Washington, from next door, had already made plans with her daughter. Our other next-door neighbors remembered that they were going to be out of town, and Nancy told me she had a headache and wasn't feeling well.

1. The Andersons said, "We are so sorry! We can't come because one of our children is sick."

2. Ms. Washington explained, ______________________________

3. The neighbors said, ______________________________

4. Nancy told Bob, ______________________________

B. Dale is talking to John about a conversation he had with Ted, the new hire:

I told him his work hadn't been up to par and that we'd hired him because of his previous experience, but we needed him to be much more proactive. I then told him that we would revisit this issue in three months and reevaluate at that point.

1. Dale said, ______________________________

____

2. Dale then said, ______________________________

____

C. Stan is talking to his brother about his girlfriend, Angie.

I told her that things had been bad for a while and that I thought we should break up. She said she knew things were bad but she thought that they would get better. I told her I wasn't sure about that, but that we could take a break and see what happened.

1. Stan said, ______________________________

____

2. Angie said, ______________________________

____

3. Stan then said, ______________________________

____

22 Practice

Rewrite the answers from Practice 17 as reported speech.

1. My grandfather often told me *that if I lay down with dogs, I'd get up with fleas.*

2. My dad often told me ______________________________.

3. My mom often told me ______________________________.

4. My brother/sister often told me ______________________________.

5. My best friend always told me ______________________________.

23 Practice

Answer the questions using reported speech.

1. What has your teacher told you about using reported speech?

   ______________________________.

2. What did your boy/girl/best friend tell you the last time you spoke?

   ______________________________.

3. Look at your last email message. Who was it from, and what did he/she say?

   ______________________________.

4. What did your house/roommate tell you last week?

   ______________________________.

5. Do you have a cell phone? Who was your last call from, and what did that person say?

   ______________________________.

6. What did the headlines in this morning's news say?

____

____.

7. What weather has the meteorologist predicted for today?

____

____.

11f Reported Speech: Questions

Student Book p. 344

24 Practice

A mother is asking her teenage daughter some questions about where she's going tonight. Read the questions, then rewrite the questions as reported speech.

1. What are you doing tonight?
2. Where is the party going to be?
3. Who is going to be there?
4. Are there going to be parents at home during the party?
5. When are you coming home?
6. Are you going to wear that?
7. Don't you have something more appropriate to wear?

Jennifer is telling her friend Mark about her mom:

1. She asked me *what I was doing tonight.*
2. ____
3. ____
4. ____
5. ____
6. ____
7. ____

25 Practice

A. You are a history teacher. Read the information on Vikings and create questions for a quiz on the reading.

The word "Viking" may come from the Swedish work *Vik* which means "bay." The Vikings were the group of people living in present day Sweden, Norway, and Denmark, who are most well known for their voyages to other countries from approximately 1060-750 B.C. The Vikings raided towns and villages across Europe, and many settled in Britain, France, and Spain. This was fairly easily done as Europe was not unified at the time. The Swedish Vikings voyaged east to Russia and the Near East, while the Danish and Norwegian Vikings went west to Europe and eventually to Iceland, Greenland, and North America.

Although many people believe they were violent, senseless, brutal people, this is just a popular misconception. Many Vikings were interested in trading and farming. Besides growing up knowing how to use a sword, Vikings were dependent on the sea for survival. The rapid attacks on unsuspecting villages were made possible by the boats the Vikings built. They were fast, long, and narrow. If there was no wind, the crew could row. They were easy to guide and could carry a large number of men.

Viking mythology states that the universe existed on a large Ash tree called "Yggdrasil," with the gods living in "Asgard" at the top of the tree, men in "Midgard," and the giants in "Jotunheim." Oden, the god of gods and men, would take the souls of men killed in battle to "Valhalla."

The age of the Vikings still captures the imagination today.

Viking Test Questions

1. Where did the Vikings come from?
2. ______________________________?
3. ______________________________?
4. ______________________________?
5. ______________________________?
6. ______________________________?
7. ______________________________?
8. ______________________________?
9. ______________________________?
10. ______________________________?
11. ______________________________?

B. Now, tell the other teachers about the test questions you asked your class.

1. I asked them where the Vikings had come from.
2. ______________________________.
3. ______________________________.
4. ______________________________.
5. ______________________________.
6. ______________________________.
7. ______________________________.
8. ______________________________.
9. ______________________________.
10. ______________________________.
11. ______________________________.

26 Practice

Jeff and Jeremy are brothers that were adopted by different families when they were young. Jeff posted a notice on an adoption search Website, and Jeremy responded. Now they're chatting online and finding out about each other. Read their dialogue and rewrite it as reported speech.

1. Jeff: I can't believe I found you! Where are you?
2. Jeremy: I live in Washington—the state. Where do you live?
3. Jeff: I live in Washington, too. I just moved here from Colorado.
4. Jeremy: Which city are you in?
5. Jeff: I'm in Seattle now. What city are you in?
6. Jeremy: I'm in Seattle, too. I live in Ballard.
7. Jeff: You are kidding me! I live there, too. What's your address?
8. Jeremy: I'm at 313 Main.
9. Jeff: No way! I can't believe it! Are you serious? Are you messing with me?
10. Jeremy: No! Of course not. Why?
11. Jeff: That's where I live.
12. Jeremy: Are you for real? What's your apartment number?
13. Jeff: I'm in 406B.
14. Jeremy: I'm in 503D. Are you at home?
15. Jeff: Yes.
16. Jeremy: I'm coming right down to meet you!

    Jeff: I'll be right here, man.

Jeremy is telling a friend about his conversation with Jeff.
Be careful! Jeremy is doing the reporting, not Jeff:

1. Jeff said he couldn't believe he'd found me and asked me where I was.
2. I told him ______________________________.
3. ______________________________.
4. ______________________________.
5. ______________________________.
6. ______________________________.

7. ______________________________.

8. ______________________________.

9. ______________________________.

10. ______________________________.

11. ______________________________.

12. ______________________________.

13. ______________________________.

14. ______________________________.

15. ______________________________.

16. ______________________________.

11g Reported Commands, Requests, Offers, Advice, Invitations, and Warnings

Student Book p. 346

27 Practice

Sylvia has started working with a personal trainer. Her trainer has given her some advice. Rewrite the direct quotations as reported commands, advice, invitations, and warnings using appropriate verbs from the list. Answers may vary.

advise	promise	tell
ask	suggest	warn
invite		

1. You should warm up every day on the treadmill for 15 minutes.

   My trainer advised me to warm up every day on the treadmill for 15 minutes.

2. It's a good idea to do some arm work every other day. ______________________________.

3. Let's focus on abs every day. ______________________________.

4. Don't push yourself too much at the beginning. ______________________________.

5. Don't continue if your knees start hurting. ______________________________

____.

6. Follow my directions carefully so you don't get hurt. ______________________

____.

7. Try drinking a glass of water before we start. ___________________________

____.

8. Please tell me if you don't understand something. _________________________

____.

9. I'm running in a marathon next month. You could come watch if you like. __________

____.

10. I will help you look and feel 100% better in just six weeks. ________________

____.

28 Practice

Joseph is telling his friends what his parents said to him last night. Write his parents' direct quotations. Answers may vary slightly.

"They are so bogus. First they warned me to stop hanging around with you guys because you're a 'bad influence'. Then they threatened to take away my computer if my grades don't improve. Get this. They offered to get me a tutor! I'm not stupid; I'm just bored. Then they warned me not to do drugs. As if! Only losers do drugs. They told me to be home at 10:30 during the week and at 12:00 on Fridays and Saturdays. I'm not a baby for crying out loud. Then, they offered to pay for college if I make these changes."

1. *"Stop hanging around friends who are a bad influence on you."*
2. ____.
3. ____.
4. ____.
5. ____.
6. ____.

29 Practice

Do you like salsa and chips? Read this recipe for homemade salsa. Then report what the recipe says to do. Use *says* and *warns* in your sentences.

from the kitchen of ______

Salsa

Put 2 large tomatoes in boiling water for 1 minute. Take them out and remove the skins. Squeeze out the seeds and cut up the flesh into small pieces. Put 1 or 2 jalapeño peppers over a gas flame or in the broiler. Don't let them burn. Take them off the flame when they turn black. Peel the jalapeños and cut them into small pieces. Remove their seeds and ribs. Wash your hands immediately. Don't touch your eyes! Peel and cut up 1 onion. Put the tomatoes, onion, and peppers into a bowl. Cut up a large clove of garlic and add to the bowl. Add some cilantro, lime juice, salt, and pepper. Serve salsa with chips. Enjoy!

1. The recipe says *to put two large tomatoes in boiling water for one minute.*
2. ______.
3. ______.
4. ______.
5. ______.
6. ______.
7. ______.
8. ______.
9. ______.

10. ____.

11. ____.

12. ____.

13. ____.

14. ____.

15. ____.

30 Practice

Mr. Hogan has had a heart attack. Write advice and warnings from his doctor.

1. Stop smoking.
2. ____.
3. ____.
4. ____.
5. ____.
6. ____.

Now rewrite the warnings as reported speech.

1. My doctor warned me to stop smoking.
2. ____.
3. ____.
4. ____.
5. ____.
6. ____.

11h The Subjunctive in Noun Clauses

Student Book p. 348

31 Practice

Read the information for an infomercial. Underline the subjunctive in noun clauses.

You have never seen a skin cream like this before, and using this line is so easy! The makers suggest that you apply the lotion once in the morning and once before bedtime for best results. We promise you will be amazed. We ask that you try the product free for 30 days, and if you decide this skin care line is not for you, we simply request that you notify us, but keep the product as our gift to you!

32 Practice

A coach is giving the team a pre-game pep talk. Write sentences using the subjunctive and the prompts.

1. owner / insist / to be out there early

   The owner insists that you be out there early.

2. fans / demand / to give 110%

   ____.

3. I / recommend / to hit them hard

   ____.

4. your teammates / expect / not to let up

   ____.

5. the offensive coach / advise / to remember their defense is weak

   ____.

6. competitive spirit / require / to go for this win

   ____.

33 Practice

Complete the sentences with your own ideas.

1. It's crucial that a child ______________________________.
2. It's vital that a police officer ______________________________.
3. It's necessary that a writer ______________________________.
4. It's important that a friend ______________________________.
5. It's desirable that a good manager ______________________________.
6. It's advisable that I ______________________________.

SELF-TEST

A Choose the best answer, A, B, C, or D, to complete the sentence. Mark your answer by darkening the oval with the same letter.

1. Have you gotten any news?

A. I'm afraid not. Ⓐ Ⓑ Ⓒ Ⓓ
B. I'm not afraid.
C. I hope so.
D. I don't hope so.

2. The clerk asked Jeff _____.

A. what does he want Ⓐ Ⓑ Ⓒ Ⓓ
B. does he want a receipt
C. if or not he wanted a receipt
D. if he wanted a receipt or not

3. Jorge said, "I'll see you later. I have to go now."

A. Jorge told he would see us later and that he had to leave then. Ⓐ Ⓑ Ⓒ Ⓓ
B. Jorge told us I will see you later and that I have to leave now.
C. Jorge told us he will see us later and that he will have to leave then.
D. Jorge told us he would see us later and that he had to leave then.

4. I asked her _____.

A. where did she get the information Ⓐ Ⓑ Ⓒ Ⓓ
B. if did she get the information
C. where she had gotten the information
D. did she get the information

5. "Please, don't do that again," said Peter.

A. Peter asked me do not do that again. Ⓐ Ⓑ Ⓒ Ⓓ
B. Peter asked me not do that again.
C. Peter asked me not to do that again.
D. Peter asked not do that again.

6. The building manager requested that ____.

A. Charles not return Ⓐ Ⓑ Ⓒ Ⓓ
B. Charles doesn't return
C. Charles didn't return
D. Charles do not return

7. "Have you finished yet?" asked Beth.

A. Beth wanted to know if I've finished yet. Ⓐ Ⓑ Ⓒ Ⓓ
B. Beth wanted to know if I'd finished yet.
C. Beth wanted to know if or not I'd finished yet.
D. Beth wanted to know I'd finished yet.

8. "I'll make dinner when I get home."

A. Junko promised she will make dinner when we get home. Ⓐ Ⓑ Ⓒ Ⓓ
B. Junko promised make dinner.
C. Junko promised to make dinner.
D. Junko promised I'll make dinner when I get home.

9. He said he didn't know who'd be there.

A. Ed said, "He didn't know who would be there." Ⓐ Ⓑ Ⓒ Ⓓ
B. Ed said, "He doesn't know who would be there."
C. Ed said, "I didn't know who will be there."
D. Ed said, "I don't know who will be there."

10. Are you finished packing?

A. I think so. Ⓐ Ⓑ Ⓒ Ⓓ
B. I'm afraid.
C. I don't hope so.
D. I don't think not.

B Find the underlined word or phrase, A, B, C, or D, that is incorrect. Mark your answer by darkening the oval with the same letter.

1. Jason said (A) me he would (B) meet us at the restaurant, but that he couldn't (C) stay (D) long.

Ⓐ Ⓑ Ⓒ Ⓓ

2. The police officer asked (A) me if or not (B) I knew (C) how fast I'd been going (D).

Ⓐ Ⓑ Ⓒ Ⓓ

3. That (A) you don't know how to do it doesn't bother (B) me, but you told (C) me you do (D).

Ⓐ Ⓑ Ⓒ Ⓓ

4. First she asked (A) me what (B) time it was, and then she asked (C) me can (D) I give her a ride.

Ⓐ Ⓑ Ⓒ Ⓓ

5. They offered (A) help (B) us move, but I told (C) them we had (D) enough people.

Ⓐ Ⓑ Ⓒ Ⓓ

6. I'm not sure (A) what do (B) they do or if (C) they have (D) jobs.

Ⓐ Ⓑ Ⓒ Ⓓ

7. Did (A) he ask (B) what's (C) your name was (D)?

Ⓐ Ⓑ Ⓒ Ⓓ

8. It's (A) urgent (B) whether (C) she is (D) at the auditorium before 8:30 tonight.

Ⓐ Ⓑ Ⓒ Ⓓ

9. Leila threatened (A) not come (B), but I offered (C) to give (D) her a ride.

Ⓐ Ⓑ Ⓒ Ⓓ

10. The mayor wasn't (A) sure whether (B) he will (C) be re-elected or not (D).

Ⓐ Ⓑ Ⓒ Ⓓ

UNIT 12 ADJECTIVE CLAUSES

12a Adjective Clauses with Subject Relative Pronouns

Student Book p. 360

1 Practice

Write sentences using the prompts and adjective clauses with *who, that,* or *which.*

1. Ally / suffer from allergies

   Ally is a woman who/that suffers from allergies.

2. athletes / exercise regularly

   ______.

3. company / allow its employees to work at home

   ______.

4. he / listen to all kinds of music

   ______.

5. laptop / use the new operating system

   ______.

6. bad drivers / run red lights and don't use their turn signals

   ______.

7. apartment / have high ceilings

   ______.

8. you (singular) / watch a lot of movies

   ______.

9. you (plural) / watch a lot of TV

   ______.

10. book / sit on the top shelf

    ______.

2 Practice

Give people in the photo names. Then complete sentences about them using adjective clauses beginning with *who* or *that*.

4. ________ 5. ________
3. ________ 6. ________
2. ________ 7. ________

1. Sherry 8. ________

1. Sherry is the woman who is sitting on the sofa.
2. ____.
3. ____.
4. ____.
5. ____.
6. ____.
7. ____.
8. ____.

12b Adjective Clauses with Object Relative Pronouns

Student Book p. 363

3 Practice

Read the sentences. Complete them with *that* if it is necessary. Leave the line blank if it is not necessary. Write if the relative pronoun is a subject or an object.

1. That's the man *that* stole my wallet. *subject*
2. It was the wallet _____ my roommate gave me. __________
3. The police officer _____ took the report eventually found my wallet. __________
4. Can I borrow the notes for the class _____ I missed today? __________
5. She's the same teacher _____ teaches art history. __________
6. Why aren't you wearing the blouse _____ you bought yesterday? __________
7. The one _____ has the red flowers? It's too hot. __________
8. No, the one _____ was in the window. __________
9. The people _____ shop at that mall must be wealthy. __________
10. I don't remember the last time _____ my roommate did the dishes. __________

4 Practice

Write sentences using the prompts, object relative pronouns, and your own ideas.

1. a bracelet / a person
   A bracelet is something that/which a person wears on his or her wrist.
2. a masterpiece / an artist
   ____.
3. a speech / a speaker ____.
4. a decision / you ____.
5. a watermelon / people ____.
6. a crown / a queen or king ____.

7. a parachute / skydivers ______________________________.

8. a water tank / a town ______________________________.

9. a landmark / travelers ______________________________.

10. a bestseller / customers ______________________________.

5 Practice

Answer the questions with your own ideas. Write complete sentences.

1. Who is the person that you admire the most? ______________________________

2. What are three areas that you'd like to improve in professionally? ______________________________

   ______________________________.

3. What is a goal that you're working toward? ______________________________

   ______________________________.

4. What's a situation that you're concerned about? ______________________________

   ______________________________.

5. What is a situation that you don't understand? ______________________________

   ______________________________.

12c Adjective Clauses with *Whose*

Student Book p. 366

6 Practice

Read the sentences. Rewrite them as two sentences.

1. My friend whose son attends the academy lives in Los Angeles.

   My friend lives in Los Angeles. His/her son attends the academy.

2. We've studied the philosopher whose ideas were revolutionary for his time. ______________________________

   ____

   ____

3. They fired the executive whose salary was the highest. ______________________________

   ____

4. She married a man whose first language is Spanish. ______________________________

   ____

5. Karina doesn't get along with some people whose politics are different from hers.

____

____

6. That's the model whose face is on every magazine cover this month. ____________

____

____

7. Justin met the neighbors whose dog keeps barking all the time. ____________

____

8. Peter is my friend whose life was saved by a kidney transplant. ____________

____

9. The jury convicted the defendant whose greed got him caught in the first place.

____

____

7 Practice

Ed Barnes is a candidate for political office. Read his speech and rewrite it using adjective clauses with *whose*. Possessive nouns and pronouns are underlined as clues.

(1) My opponent's attitude bothers me. (2) His lack of foresight has lead this country into near bankruptcy. (3) His continued disregard for the public's welfare is shocking and his denials of any wrongdoing trouble me, and they should trouble you.

(4) My only interest is seeing everyone in this community enjoying economic prosperity. (5) My leadership skills will move us to that end. (6) My team of experts has assured me that we have a very good chance of beating the incumbent.

(7) Your opinion matters to me. Remember to vote in this next election. (8) Your vote is very important.

1. *I am running against an opponent whose attitude* .
2. ____.

3. ____.

4. ____.

5. ____.

6. ____.

7. ____.

8. ____.

8 Practice

When Joe left the office this afternoon, he discovered that someone had let the air out of his tires. Read about his coworkers. Write two sentences for each, saying if he or she may have or may not have done it. Use *whose* or subject or object relative pronouns in the adjective clauses.

1. Woman #1 - can't stand Joe because she was his temporary supervisor and trained Joe for the job. When he became her supervisor, he fired her. Her last day was today.

   The woman who was fired may have done it because she's angry. (OR)

   The woman who trained Joe may have done it because she's angry.

2. Man #1 - doesn't like Joe because today he yelled at him in front of the other team members, which was unnecessary, especially considering he had recently loaned Joe $100. He's been in his office since early this morning.

   ____.

   ____.

3. Woman #2 - doesn't respect Joe because he took credit for a project she completed. Today, she missed an important conference call because he told her it was scheduled one hour later.

   ____.

   ____.

4. Man #2 - is angry with Joe because when he came back from vacation yesterday, Joe had taken one of his main accounts. Additionally, Joe asked him to work late this afternoon, but Joe left the office early.

   ____.

   ____.

9 Practice

What qualities and characteristics do you look for in a friend? Write sentences with adjective clauses using *whose* and words from the list or your own ideas.

age	ideas	physical appearance
background	income	sense of humor
educational level	job	values

1. I like people whose values are similar to my own.
2. ______________________________.
3. ______________________________.
4. ______________________________.
5. ______________________________.
6. ______________________________.
7. ______________________________.
8. ______________________________.
9. ______________________________.

12d *When, Where, Why,* and *That* as Relative Pronouns

Student Book p. 368

10 Practice

Lucy and Dirk are showing photos and telling their neighbors about a trip. Read their sentences and combine them in two ways: once using *where* and once using *that* + *in, at, on,* or *to*.

1. We visited the battlefield. Thousands of soldiers died there.

   a. We visited the battlefield where thousands of soldiers died.

   b. We visited the battlefield that thousands of soldiers died on.

2. We saw the house. The religious leader was born there.

   ______________________________.

   ______________________________.

3. This is the clock tower. We had our picture taken there.

______________________________.

______________________________.

4. We chose a small town. Fewer tourists were there.

______________________________.

______________________________.

5. We stayed at a hotel. The royal family had stayed there the week before.

______________________________.

______________________________.

6. This is the restaurant. Our friends took us there.

______________________________.

______________________________.

7. This is the square. We lost our traveler's checks there.

______________________________.

______________________________.

8. Next year we'd like to go to a place. The weather is a little warmer.

______________________________.

______________________________.

II Practice

Complete the sentences with *when* and your own ideas.

1. That was the birthday *when my uncle fell into the pool.*
2. Do you remember the year ______________________________?
3. The night ______________________________ was terrible.
4. I'll never forget the time ______________________________.
5. The New Year's Eve ______________________________ was a lot of fun.
6. My most memorable experience was the summer ______________________________.

12 Practice

Combine the sentences in two ways using *when, where, that,* or *why*. You may use prepositions with *that*.

1. That was the party. I met my wife.

   That was the party where I met my wife.

   That was the party that I met my wife at.

2. It was the fall. I started teaching at the university.

   ______________________________.

   ______________________________.

3. We got married in the same place. We met there.

   ______________________________.

   ______________________________.

4. That is the reason. We went to the same place on our second honeymoon.

   ______________________________.

   ______________________________.

5. We moved to the city. Her family is there.

   ______________________________.

   ______________________________.

6. It is the reason. We moved to the city.

   ______________________________.

   ______________________________.

13 Practice

Answer the questions. Use *why* in your adjective clause.

1. What's the reason (why) people go to war? ______________________________.
2. What's the reason (why) people should be concerned about the environment?

   ______________________________.
3. Do you know the reason (why) the moon looks larger at the horizon than when it rises? ______________________________.
4. What's the reason (why) you're studying English? ______________________________.

12e Defining and Nondefining Adjective Clauses

Student Book p. 371

14 Practice

Read the sentences. Write *D* next to the sentence if the adjective clause is defining. Write *ND* if the adjective clause is nondefining.

_____ **1.** Lilacs, which are my mother's favorite flower, don't grow well in this climate.

_____ **2.** The lilacs which mom planted last year are just starting to bloom.

_____ **3.** Whole wheat bread, which is bread that has a lot of natural fiber, is good for you.

_____ **4.** The whole wheat bread that's made in that bakery is kind of expensive, but delicious.

_____ **5.** Children who don't eat breakfast don't do as well in school as those who do.

_____ **6.** Children, who need good nutrition to do well in school, have a lot more homework these days than in the past.

_____ **7.** The paper which is used to print photos is more expensive than regular printer paper.

_____ **8.** Paper, which is made from wood pulp and various chemicals, is processed in paper mills.

_____ **9.** Antique jewelry, which is jewelry 100 years old or older, can be expensive to buy.

_____ **10.** The antique necklace that my grandmother gave me needs to be repaired.

15 Practice

Read the statements. Underline the subject.

1. Toys, which can help children learn, have changed dramatically in the last 100 years.

2. Toys that have very small parts should not be given to very young children.

3. Guacamole, which is made from avocados, lime, cilantro, garlic, salt, and pepper, is very popular in Mexican restaurants.

4. The guacamole which my husband makes is out of this world!

5. The grammar exercises which are in this book are fun and easy!

6. Grammar exercises, which are designed to help people learn language, involve rules.

7. Garlic, which some people believe has medical properties, is easy to grow.

8. The garlic which you can buy crushed in a jar has a different taste from fresh garlic.

16 Practice

Underline and put commas around the nondefining adjective clauses.

Some of the earliest ways to measure time were the use of obelisks in Egypt. Obelisks which are tall four-sided towers cast shadows which people could use to measure different times of day. Later, people used water clocks which measured time by how long it took for water to leak from one container to another. Water clocks which didn't depend on the sun, moon, or stars had markings in them to indicate time periods as the containers filled with the water. Candles which were also used to mark the passage of time burned to marks made along the side. In the 1400s, mechanical clocks which use a mainspring and balance wheel were introduced. In 1657, Christiaan Huygens built the first clock that used a pendulum. In 1884, many countries adopted Greenwich, England, as the Prime Meridian which indicates zero degrees longitude. In the 1920s, quartz clocks were developed. Quartz crystals which can produce regular electric pulses were found to be more accurate in keeping time than clocks which contained gears.

12f Using *Which* to Refer to an Entire Clause

Student Book p. 374

17 Practice

Combine the sentences with *which*.

1. Martha is in really good shape. This makes her happy.

   Martha is in really good shape, which makes her happy ______.

2. Martha's running partner, Julia, has entered them in a triathlon for this fall. This has surprised Martha. ______________________________

   ______________________________.

3. Martha and Julia are going to have only five months to train before the triathlon. This makes Martha a little nervous. ______________________________

   ______________________________.

4. She and Julia have run races together, but they haven't done the swimming or cycling before. This worries her. ______________________________

   ______________________________.

5. Julia has done several triathlons. This is why she knows that they can do it.

   ______________________________.

6. Martha is an excellent swimmer. This will be when she makes good time in the race. ______________________________

   ______________________________.

7. Julia has organized training rides to get Martha ready for the cycling part of the race. This will build Martha's cycling stamina. ______________________________

   ______________________________.

8. After the triathlon, they are going to take a vacation for two weeks. This is just long enough to recover! ______________________________

   ______________________________.

18 Practice

Complete the sentences with *which* and your own ideas.

1. He had to drive for 12 hours, which was exhausting. ______
2. We didn't have enough sugar for the cake, ______________________________.
3. Our goldfish died, ______________________________.

4. No one talked to us at the reception, ______________________________.

5. The mechanic said the repair would cost $900.00, ______________________________.

6. The doctor said there was nothing seriously wrong, ______________________________.

7. My daughter wants to play the drums, ______________________________.

8. Jeff made my favorite dessert, ______________________________.

9. No one was hurt in the accident, ______________________________.

10. My company is eliminating our medical insurance, ______________________________.

19 Practice

Complete the sentences with your own ideas.

1. I ____________________, which ____________________.
2. My friends ____________________, which ____________________.
3. My parents ____________________, which ____________________.
4. My grandfather ____________________, which ____________________.
5. My teacher ____________________, which ____________________.

12g Reduced Adjective Clauses

Student Book p. 376

20 Practice

Underline the reduced adjective clauses (the adjective phrases).

Before the existence of money, barter, the exchange of goods and services for other goods and services, was the primary means of acquisition. In China, from approximately 9000 to 6000 B.C., cattle and grain were used for barter. From about 1200 B.C., many cultures used cowry shells, the shell from an animal found in the Pacific and Indian Oceans. This practice lasted for many hundreds of years. In 1000 B.C., China started producing coins made of metal, typically having a hole in them so as to be put on a string. In the country of Lydia, now part of Turkey, the first modern coins, made from silver and having a round shape, were manufactured. In China in 118 B.C., leather money appeared. This leather strip was the predecessor for paper notes, also appearing for the first time in China. In North America in the 1500s, "wampum," strings of shell beads, was used by the Native Americans for trade, as gifts, and other purposes. In later years, England and the United States adopted the gold standard, abandoned in the United States after the Great Depression. Today people rely on bank cards representing how much money a person has for many of their daily transactions.

21 Practice

Reduce the adjective clauses. Rewrite the sentences.

1. On November 7, 1940, the Tacoma Narrows Bridge, which was the third longest bridge in the world, collapsed after only four months.

   On November 7, 1940, the Tacoma Narrows Bridge, the third longest bridge in the world, collapsed after only four months.

2. The bridge, which was located on the Tacoma Narrows, was light and flexible.

   ____

   ______________________________.

3. The bridge, which was called "Galloping Gertie," would move when the wind blew at relatively low speeds.

____

____.

4. No one thought the bridge, which had been designed by a well-known engineer, was dangerous.

____

____.

5. On November 7, 1940, the wind, which had a speed of about 42 miles per hour, caused the bridge to oscillate violently.

____

____.

6. The people who were driving in the two cars that were on the bridge at the time of its collapse got away safely.

____

____.

7. The collapse, which was seen and documented by many people, taught engineers about the unique properties of suspension bridges.

____

____.

22 Practice

Expand the reduced adjective clauses.

1. People thinking about going on a low-carb diet should talk to their doctors first.

   People who are thinking about going on a low-carb diet should talk to their doctors first.

2. The light coming into the west window keeps the living room warm in the afternoon.

____

____.

3. People unhappy in their current careers should seek advice from a counselor.

____.

4. Do you see the men talking on the corner? The one on the right is my boss.

____.

____.

5. Buildings built before the 1900s are protected under landmark status in this town.

____

____.

6. I can't eat products made with peanuts.

____.

7. My dad doesn't listen to any music recorded after 1990.

____.

8. Merchants selling jewelry on the street must have a permit.

____.

9. Does anyone know what happened to the money left on the table?

____.

10. The people living in the downstairs apartment just moved out.

____.

23 Practice

Complete the sentences with your own ideas.

1. Shoes made in Italy *are of a very good quality.*
2. Music coming out of Europe these days ______________________.
3. Movies from Hollywood ______________________.
4. Soccer players making a lot of money______________________.
5. A car alarm going off in the middle of the night ______________________.
6. Cars consuming a lot of gasoline ______________________.
7. People downloading music from the Internet ______________________.
8. Teenagers using drugs ______________________.
9. Tourists looking for an interesting place to visit ______________________.
10. Tea grown in Japan ______________________.

SELF-TEST

A Choose the best answer, A, B, C, or D, to complete the sentence. Mark your answer by darkening the oval with the same letter.

1. I have a friend _____ son is on TV.

A. who (A) (B) (C) (D)
B. whose
C. that
D. when

2. We just passed the hospital _____ I was born.

A. where (A) (B) (C) (D)
B. which
C. that
D. when

3. Sunset is the time _____ the birds are their most active.

A. where (A) (B) (C) (D)
B. which
C. that
D. when

4. Calendars are tools _____ track the passage of time.

A. where (A) (B) (C) (D)
B. who
C. that
D. when

5. The typewriter, _____ was the predecessor to the modern word processor, was invented in 1873.

A. where (A) (B) (C) (D)
B. who
C. that
D. which

6. Donald doesn't have a computer, _____ puts him at a disadvantage with his coworkers.

A. where (A) (B) (C) (D)
B. who
C. that
D. which

7. The house _____ was broken into last Saturday night.

A. at the end of the block (A) (B) (C) (D)
B. where at the end of the block
C. that at the end of the block
D. which at the end of the block

8. I love the smell of bread _____ in the oven.

A. bakes (A) (B) (C) (D)
B. which bake
C. that bake
D. baking

9. Stan prefers watching films _____ Japan.

A. where (A) (B) (C) (D)
B. whose
C. that are from
D. which

10. The bus _____ now is an express one. You can get downtown in 20 minutes.

A. come (A) (B) (C) (D)
B. coming
C. that come
D. which come

B Find the underlined word or phrase, A, B, C, or D, that is incorrect. Mark your answer by darkening the oval with the same letter.

1. Lava lamps, _that were loved in the 1960s_ A, _are_ B popular again. _People nostalgic for the past_ C may invest in _one of these_ D retro items.

   (A) (B) (C) (D)

2. The Suez Canal, _which links_ A two seas, may have _been planned_ B in ancient Egypt. The idea was revisited by Napoleon, _who_ C engineers made calculations, later _found_ D to be faulty.

   (A) (B) (C) (D)

3. Apples _sold_ A in the supermarket don't taste as good as those _who_ B _sold_ C _at an_ D orchard.

   (A) (B) (C) (D)

4. The campground _when_ A we spent our last vacation _was destroyed_ B by a tornado _that_ C _touched down_ D last week.

   (A) (B) (C) (D)

5. My dad, _who's_ A not feeling well, just _called_ B me. His leg, _injuring_ C when he fell down last year, was _bothering_ D him.

   (A) (B) (C) (D)

6. Shrimp, also _known_ A as prawns, are high in cholesterol. Patients _telling_ B to lower their cholesterol levels by their doctors, may _have to_ C avoid _eating_ D shrimp.

   (A) (B) (C) (D)

7. Mt. Rushmore, _which_ A is _locating_ B in South Dakota, _is_ C _visited_ D by tourists every year.

   (A) (B) (C) (D)

8. The terms _agreed_ A to last year have been _changed_ B to reflect the cost of living. This increase, _which_ C was 1.5%, has negatively impacted manufacturing, _that_ D is bad news.

   (A) (B) (C) (D)

9. Our professor, _whose_ A usually very busy, _stayed_ B after class to answer questions _that_ C we _had_ D about our test tomorrow.

   (A) (B) (C) (D)

10. Peach Melba, a dessert _named_ A for an opera singer, _was created_ B by Escoffier. The dessert, _made_ C from peaches, was one of two food items _naming_ D for the singer.

    (A) (B) (C) (D)

UNIT 13 ADVERB CLAUSES

13a Adverb Clauses of Time

Student Book p. 390

1 Practice

Read the short passages about successful individuals. Then match the sentence halves to create complete sentences about their lives.

A.

Phil Barsky is a filmmaker who has recently had some success. His new film *Alone* was just nominated for an Academy Award. The awards will be presented next week, and critics predict that Barsky will be taking home an Oscar. Barsky hasn't always been so successful, however. The film *Alone* was what made people finally pay attention to him. In the past, he has made small movies that failed at the box office or that were never released. His new film suggests he has come a long way from his days as a production assistant. He has come an even longer way from his previous job: he used to be a dishwasher at Planet Hollywood in Los Angeles!

_____	**1.** When the Academy Awards are presented next week,	**a.** before he made movies.
_____	**2.** Until he made the movie *Alone,*	**b.** he was a production assistant.
_____	**3.** Barsky was a dishwasher at Planet Hollywood	**c.** they failed at the box office.
_____	**4.** Before he was a filmmaker,	**d.** Barsky may win an Oscar.
_____	**5.** Whenever he released his previous movies,	**e.** nobody paid attention to Barsky's work.

B.

In her childhood, Dr. Leslie Thorne was always fascinated by outer space. She used to look at the moon and the stars through a telescope that her father had given her for her tenth birthday. In high school, she took the most advanced math and science classes, and her teachers encouraged her to study astronomy and physics in college. Dr. Thorne worked hard, studied for many years, and earned a Ph.D. in astronomy. Her Ph.D. research was published last year. Immediately after that, she was asked to join an expedition in space as a researcher. She will accompany a crew of scientists on a research mission at the next shuttle launch, scheduled for June 15, 2005.

_____	**1.** When Dr. Thorne was a girl,	**a.** when she turned ten.
_____	**2.** Her father gave her a telescope	**b.** Dr. Thorne was offered an opportunity to join a research team in space.
_____	**3.** Dr. Thorne took the most advanced math and science classes	**c.** when she went to college.
_____	**4.** Dr. Thorne studied astronomy and physics	**d.** while she was in high school.
_____	**5.** After Dr. Thorne finished her Ph.D.,	**e.** she was very interested in outer space.
_____	**6.** As soon as her Ph.D. research was published,	**f.** Dr. Thorne will be there with a research team.
_____	**7.** The next time that a space shuttle is launched,	**g.** her research was published.

2 Practice

Read the sentences. Write *C* next to the sentence if it uses the adverb clause of time correctly. Write *I* if it uses the adverb clause of time incorrectly. Then correct the sentences with errors. There may be more than one way to correct an error.

_____ **1.** As soon as you get home please give me a call.

____.

_____ **2.** Their car will be repaired by the time they return.

____.

_____ **3.** As long as we have enough water, we will feel fine on our hike.

____.

_____ **4.** Were you worried the first time when you traveled alone?

____?

_____ **5.** Whenever I saw that movie the first time, I was very scared.

____.

_____ **6.** The workers may go home only until the job is finished.

____.

_____ **7.** Amy has gone to the theater every weekend, since she moved to New York.

____.

_____ **8.** Once they get married, they will look for a house.

____.

_____ **9.** While Susan was talking on the phone, when her dog ran out the door.

____.

_____ **10.** Everyone watched in horror, as the dancer fell off the stage.

____.

3 Practice

Who do you think is successful? Write a paragraph about someone's accomplishments. The person can be someone you know personally or someone who is famous. Use at least six adverb clauses of time.

____

____

____

____

____

____

____

____

____

13b Adverb Clauses of Reason and Result

Student Book p. 393

4 Practice

Complete the sentences by circling the correct words in parentheses. Pay attention to punctuation.

1. Yesterday I took the subway to work (so / because) my car was being repaired at the garage.
2. I planned an extra thirty minutes to get to work (so / because) the subway can be slow in the morning.
3. A lot of people take the subway to work, (so / because) the busiest time to travel is between 7:00 and 8:00 A.M.
4. The subway was almost full, (so / because) many people didn't have seats.
5. The subway stopped in the tunnel (so / because) there was a mechanical problem.

6. The tunnel was dark and the subway lights didn't work; (because / consequently) some people started to get worried.

7. Twenty minutes went by; (as a result / because of), some people started to look at their watches.

8. We were in a tunnel, (so / therefore) I couldn't call my boss on my cell phone to tell him I would be late.

9. Like the other people on the train, I was upset (because / because of) the long delay.

10. Eventually a repair car came; (therefore / so) the train was fixed and we arrived at the next station.

5 Practice

Rewrite each pair of sentences in two ways, once using *so ... that* and once using *such (a/an) ... that*.

1. Erin and Paul dined at a new restaurant. Almost nobody else was there.
   a. *The restaurant was so new that almost nobody else was there.*
   b. *It was such a new restaurant that almost nobody else was there.*

2. The service was slow. They waited thirty minutes for their food.
   a. ______________________________
   ____
   b. ______________________________
   ____

3. The view was beautiful. Erin and Paul didn't mind the slow service.
   a. ______________________________
   b. ______________________________

4. The afternoon was warm. They did not need to wear jackets.

   a. ____________________

   b. ____________________

5. The pasta was delicious. They ate every bite of it.

   a. ____________________

   b. ____________________

6. The dessert was sweet. Erin couldn't eat all of it.

   a. ____________________

   b. ____________________

7. The bill was expensive. Paul thought there must be a mistake.

   a. ____________________

   b. ____________________

8. The restaurant was romantic. Erin and Paul decided to eat there again someday.

   a. ____________________

   b. ____________________

6 Practice

Add the correct punctuation to each sentence. For some sentences, there may be more than one way to add punctuation. Some sentences may not need punctuation.

1. The firefighter was very brave and so he won an award.
2. Since I must go to work so early I decided to go to bed early.
3. Gil didn't understand his math homework therefore he found a math tutor.
4. Rick was upset because his brother lost his favorite tie.
5. My sister is allergic to bees as a result she has to carry medicine with her.
6. Because of the earthquake many homes were damaged.
7. It was such a long class that the students had difficulty paying attention.
8. Our flight was delayed and as a result we did not leave until the next day.
9. Beth bought the wrong size dress so she'll have to return to the store.
10. The company had to close consequently many people lost their jobs.

13c Adverb Clauses of Purpose

Student Book p. 397

7 Practice

Circle the letter of the sentence that uses an adverb clause of purpose.

1. **a.** The book was so good that I read it twice.

   b. I read the book twice so that I would remember it better.

2. **a.** I'm going to study hard so that I'll be prepared for the test.

   b. I studied so hard that I was very well prepared for the test.

3. **a.** I set the alarm clock so early that I woke up long before the test.

   b. I set the alarm clock so that I would wake up very early on the day of the test.

4. **a.** At lunch, I was so hungry that I ate two sandwiches.

   b. At lunch, I ate two sandwiches so that I wouldn't be hungry anymore.

5. **a.** Jess bought a lot of groceries so that she wouldn't have to go shopping for a long time.

   b. Jess bought so many groceries that she didn't have to go shopping for a long time.

6. **a.** Mike worked so quickly that he was able to go home early.

   b. Mike worked quickly so that he could go home early.

8 Practice

Complete the sentences with *in order to* or *so that* to show purpose, or *therefore* to show result. Add commas, semicolons, and periods where necessary.

Mariel bought a new handbag, but when she got home, she saw that the strap was broken. ___Therefore___ (1), she decided to take it back to the store. She put the sales receipt in her pocket ________ (2) she could show when she bought the bag and how much she paid for it. At the store, she showed the salesclerk the broken strap. She said she had brought the bag back ________ (3) replace it with a different one. The salesclerk said she needed the receipt ________ (4) approve the exchange. Mariel looked in her pocket, but she couldn't find the receipt. Then she noticed there was a hole in her pocket ________ (5) the receipt must have fallen out somewhere. Mariel walked back to the entrance of the store, looking at the ground ________ (6) she might see the lost receipt. At last she found it just outside the door. She ran back to the salesclerk in order to give her the receipt before she lost it again. ______(7)______, the salesclerk was able to exchange the handbag, and Mariel found one without a broken strap. Now whenever she buys something, she puts the sales receipt in her new handbag ______(8)______ she doesn't lose it.

9 Practice

Have you ever lost something or worried about losing something? Write a paragraph of at least six sentences about your experience. Use *in order to* or *so that* to show purpose and *therefore, as a result,* or *consequently* to show result. Use the correct punctuation.

Example: *Last summer, I was the best man in my brother's wedding. My brother gave me the wedding rings so that I would be able to present them during the ceremony. I put them in my jacket pocket in order to keep them safe. . .*

____

____

____

____

____

____

____

____

____

____

____

____

13d Adverb Clauses of Contrast

Student Book p. 399

10 Practice

Circle the correct adverb in parentheses to complete the sentences.

Every January, (when / because of)[1] the ground is covered with snow and the trees are glistening with ice, our city has a Winter Festival. For three days, people come to the city center (so that / in order to)[2] play winter games, ice skate on the pond, and view the amazing ice sculptures. The ice sculptures are the most famous part of the Winter Festival (though / because)[3] they are made by famous sculptors from different countries. Some of the sculptures are impressive (even though / because of)[4] their large size, (whereas / although)[5] others are smaller but show amazing detail. For example, one sculpture of a house was very simple; (however / whereas)[6], it was large enough to walk in. Another sculpture I remember was of a Japanese fan that was small (so that / though)[7] detailed.

(So that / Therefore)[8] the artists can make their sculptures, the weather conditions need to be just right. (Once / Although)[9] the temperature rises above freezing, it becomes very difficult to make ice sculptures. In addition, the sculptures don't last long (nevertheless / when)[10] the air gets warmer or it rains. Unfortunately, last year this is exactly what happened. The day (before / until)[11] the festival started, it was 40 degrees Fahrenheit. (Even though / Because of)[12] the warm temperature, the sculptures started to melt. Some were melting (consequently / while)[13] the artists were still trying to finish them. Snow machines were brought to the park, as well as fans blowing cold air (so that / however)[14] the ice wouldn't melt so quickly. Tents were constructed (in order to / because of)[15] keep the rain off the sculptures. These efforts weren't enough, (even though / though)[16]. The ice continued to melt. (So that / Therefore)[17], everyone worried that there would be no ice sculptures at the festival.

On the second day of the festival, it got even warmer. (Whereas / Although) it rained steadily for the next day and a half, people came to the Winter Festival anyway. The ice artists displayed photographs of their sculptures (nevertheless / so that) people could see something interesting. (However / While) everyone missed seeing the real ice sculptures, most people agreed that it was nice to see the photographs. It was disappointing not to have winter weather; (whereas / nevertheless), most people had fun anyway.

18 19 20 21

11 Practice

Combine each pair of sentences into one longer sentence using the adverbs in parentheses. Use the correct punctuation.

1. My city, Montreal, is very cold in the winter. There are many fun things to do outside. (although, however)

   a. *Although my city is very cold in the winter, there are many fun things to do outside.*

   b. ______________________________

2. You can go ice-skating in the park. Sometimes it is too cold for that. (although, nevertheless)

   a. ______________________________

   b. ______________________________

3. Many people like to go shopping in the underground malls. Others prefer visiting museums. (while, though)

   a. ______________________________

   b. ______________________________

4. The streets can be slippery with ice. Some people think it's romantic to ride in a horse and carriage. (even though, however)

a. ______________________________

____

b. ______________________________

____

5. It's a long drive. It's fun to go to Quebec City for the winter festival. (although, nevertheless)

a. ______________________________

____

b. ______________________________

____

6. My husband always wants to go somewhere warmer in the winter. I prefer to stay in Canada. (whereas, though)

a. ______________________________

____

b. ______________________________

____

12 Practice

Study the pairs of photographs. Write at least four sentences about the differences between them using adverb clauses of contrast *although, even though, though, whereas, while, nevertheless,* and *however*. Use the correct punctuation.

A.

____

____

____

____

____

B.

____

____

____

____

____

13e Adverb Clauses of Condition

Student Book p. 401

13 Practice

Rewrite the sentences using the words in parentheses. Use the correct punctuation.

Vinnie's Wraps:

Employee's Handbook

1. If it is not a special promotion day, all employees must wear black pants and a green shirt to work. (unless)

   Unless it is a special promotion day, all employees must wear black pants and a green shirt to work.

2. Whether or not you washed your hands before coming to work, you must wash them again before handling food. (even if)

   ____

   ____

3. Hair must be tied back and worn under a cap if it isn't above your shoulders. (unless)

   ____

   ____

4. Personal phone calls are not permitted unless it is an emergency. (only if)

   ____

   ____

5. You should talk to your supervisor if you have problems with your schedule. (in case)

   ____

   ____

6. All requests for vacation time must be in writing; it does not matter if you have talked to your supervisor first. (whether or not)

   ____

   ____

7. You may have one free meal on your shift. This is true if you work only a five-hour shift. (even if)

____

____

8. Food can only be consumed in the employee kitchen; however, if the restaurant is closed, you may eat in the dining room. (unless)

____

____

14 Practice

Rewrite the sentences two ways with *only if*. The first time, use the *only if* clause in the second part of the sentence. The second time, use the *only if* clause at the beginning of the sentence. Use the correct punctuation.

1. I can buy a used car. In order to do so, I have to save $2,000.

   a. I can buy a used car only if I save $2,000.

   b. Only if I save $2,000 can I buy a used car.

2. I can save $2,000. In order to do so, I must stop buying things I don't need.

   a. ____

   b. ____

3. I will stop buying lunch every day. The only way I can do that is to make my lunch at home.

   a. ____

   b. ____

4. I will quit drinking expensive coffee. But I can't do that unless I stop walking past that new cafe on my way to work.

   a. ____

   b. ____

5. I will cancel my cable TV service. The only way to do that is to start reading more.

   a. ____

   b. ____

6. I can get books from the library instead of the bookstore. But I can't do this until I pay my library fine.

   a. ______________________________

   b. ______________________________

7. I'll stop using my cell phone so often. To do so, my friends will need to start calling me at home.

   a. ______________________________

   b. ______________________________

8. I could just get a second job—but I would need to have a car in order to get from one job to the other.

   a. ______________________________

   b. ______________________________

15 Practice

What rules did you have to follow when you were growing up, or what rules must you live by now? Did your parents or an older sibling make rules for you? Write six rules using adverb clauses of condition. Use the correct punctuation.

Example: *When I was growing up, my older brother was very bossy. I couldn't watch a TV show unless it was a show that he liked. I could play with him and his friends only if he was in a good mood. Even if I was very nice to him, he teased me. Only if I cried did he stop and apologize.*

____

____

____

____

____

____

____

____

____

13f Reduced Adverb Clauses

Student Book p. 404

16 Practice

Read the sentences. Write *AC* next to the sentence if an adverb clause is used. Write *AP* if an adverb phrase is used.

_____ **1.** After living in their apartment for two years, Carl and Adene decided to make some changes.

_____ **2.** Wanting to make some inexpensive changes, they decided to paint the walls.

_____ **3.** Before they started the project, they looked at magazines to see what colors they liked.

_____ **4.** When they looked at paint, the amount of choices they had suddenly became overwhelming.

_____ **5.** After they argued over different colors, they finally agreed to paint two walls of the living room blue and two walls yellow.

_____ **6.** They prepared the walls with white primer before applying colored paint.

_____ **7.** While painting, Adene secretly worried that the colors would look bad.

_____ **8.** Once the walls were painted, however, Adene realized that blue and yellow looked good together.

_____ **9.** Since they redecorated the living room, they have gone on to change the kitchen.

_____ **10.** Because they know how to paint a room, the job will probably go faster now.

17 Practice

Rewrite the sentences in Practice 16. Change adverb phrases to adverb clauses. Reduce adverb clauses to adverb phrases. If a clause cannot be reduced, write *can't reduce.*

1. After they had lived in their apartment for two years, Carl and Adene decided to make some changes.
2. ______________________
3. ______________________
4. ______________________
5. ______________________
6. ______________________
7. ______________________
8. ______________________
9. ______________________
10. ______________________

18 Practice

Read the sentences. Write *C* next to the sentence if the adverb clause or phrase is used correctly. Write *I* if it is used incorrectly.

______ **1.** Because wanting to do some research, Tom went to the library.

______ **2.** When finished, this painting will sell for over $10,000.

______ **3.** Since she beginning violin lessons, Yushen has learned six songs.

______ **4.** Can you stop at the hardware store before returned home?

______ **5.** The Robertsons talked to their son upon they learned he had failed physics.

______ **6.** Make sure you have all the ingredients before cooking this meal.

______ **7.** After listened to loud music at the concert, I decided that I should wear earplugs.

______ **8.** I can't study while watching TV.

19 Practice

Write a paragraph of instructions about how to make or do something. Use one of the ideas from the list or an idea of your own. Use at least six reduced adverb clauses.

How to boil an egg

How to download music

How to make coffee

How to place an international phone call

How to use email

____

____

____

____

____

____

____

____

____

____

SELF-TEST

A Choose the best answer, A, B, C, or D, to complete the sentence. Mark your answer by darkening the oval with the same letter.

1. _______ Ed has traveled all over Latin America, he has never been to Brazil.

A. Because (A) (B) (C) (D)
B. However
C. Although
D. So that

2. The car was _______ expensive that we couldn't consider buying it.

A. such (A) (B) (C) (D)
B. such an
C. too
D. so

3. _______ Mr. Benson returns, I will give him your message.

A. Until (A) (B) (C) (D)
B. While
C. Once
D. Before

4. You should look on the Internet _______ find the best deal on a car.

A. in order that (A) (B) (C) (D)
B. in order to
C. so that
D. so to

5. You should take money for a taxi _______ you think you won't need it.

A. in case (A) (B) (C) (D)
B. even if
C. whether or not
D. only if

6. Muriel gets angry _______ she is interrupted at work.

A. whenever (A) (B) (C) (D)
B. since
C. the next time
D. so long as

7. Because of _______, school was cancelled for the day.

A. the snow (A) (B) (C) (D)
B. it was snowing
C. it snowed
D. snowing

8. Jim called the phone company _______ he could have his phone repaired.

A. such that (A) (B) (C) (D)
B. in order to
C. so that
D. because of

9. The skier broke her leg; _______, she didn't compete.

A. however (A) (B) (C) (D)
B. as a result
C. until
D. because of

10. It's dangerous to talk on the phone _______ driving a car.

A. you are (A) (B) (C) (D)
B. while you
C. while
D. while are

B Find the underlined word or phrase, A, B, C, or D, that is incorrect. Mark your answer by darkening the oval with the same letter.

1. Upon learn (A) the good news, I called (B) all my friends in order (C) to tell them (D).

Ⓐ Ⓑ Ⓒ Ⓓ

2. We forgot to lock (A) the door behind us (B) the last time (C) left (D) the building.

Ⓐ Ⓑ Ⓒ Ⓓ

3. As soon as (A) you have (B) the time, you need to sign (C) the form in order we (D) refund your money.

Ⓐ Ⓑ Ⓒ Ⓓ

4. Because it was (A) so bad TV show (B), it was cancelled (C) after only three shows.

Ⓐ Ⓑ Ⓒ Ⓓ

5. The employees won't be satisfied (A) however (B) they are paid fairly (C) for their work (D).

Ⓐ Ⓑ Ⓒ Ⓓ

6. Some people love hot weather, whereas (A) some people can't stand to be (B) in the summer heat in case (C) they have (D) an air conditioner.

Ⓐ Ⓑ Ⓒ Ⓓ

7. As a result (A) it hadn't rained (B) for many weeks (C), wildfires were destroying (D) the forests.

Ⓐ Ⓑ Ⓒ Ⓓ

8. Whether or not (A) it rains (B), we should take (C) the umbrellas on our picnic so we will be that prepared for anything.

Ⓐ Ⓑ Ⓒ Ⓓ

9. My sister, who loves music (A), cannot sing very well (B); consequently (C), she was asked to be (D) the lead singer in a band.

Ⓐ Ⓑ Ⓒ Ⓓ

10. I'll help you (A) with your English homework only if (B) help me (C) to study for (D) the math test.

Ⓐ Ⓑ Ⓒ Ⓓ

UNIT 14 CONDITIONAL SENTENCES

14a Real Conditional Sentences in the Present and Future

Student Book p. 416

1 Practice

Match the sentences with the functions of the present real conditional.

Functions of the Present Real Conditional
a. To say that something always happens in a specific situation.
b. To talk about a general fact that is always true.
c. To talk about something that may possibly happen in the future (but also may not).
d. To suggest less certainty about the condition.
e. To tell someone to do something (imperative).

_____ **1.** If you want to make a call, please hang up and dial again.

_____ **2.** If you are trying to reach Ms. Landry, she is out of the office on Mondays.

_____ **3.** If you do not press "one" after leaving a message, your message will not be sent.

_____ **4.** If you should need to speak with someone immediately, please call Denise Williamson at extension 4573.

_____ **5.** If you leave a message, Ms. Landry will return your call as soon as possible.

2 Practice

Rewrite the sentences in Practice 1 with the conditional clause at the end of the sentence.

1. ____________________
2. ____________________
3. ____________________
4. ____________________
5. ____________________

3 Practice

Give someone advice about visiting your city or country. Use the present real conditional and add the correct punctuation. Write two sentences for each question.

1. What is something that always happens to visitors in your city or country?

   If people visit my (city / country), they ____________________.

   People ____________________ if ____________________.

2. What is a general fact about your city or country?

   If ____________________, ____________________.

   ____________________ if ____________________.

3. What is something that may or may not happen to visitors there?

   If ____________________, ____________________.

   ____________________ if ____________________.

4. What is a situation that you're not sure about, and what is the possible result?

   If visitors should ____________________, they ____________________.

   ____________________ if they should ____________________.

5. What is the most important advice you have for visitors? (Use an imperative in the main clause).

   If ____________________, ____________________.

   ____________________ if ____________________.

14b Unreal Conditional Sentences in the Present or Future

Student Book p. 419

4 Practice

Kimberly is supposed to give a speech in her English class tomorrow. Rewrite the real present conditionals as unreal present conditionals.

1. If Kimberly practices her speech tonight, she won't be nervous tomorrow.

   If Kimberly practiced her speech tonight, she wouldn't be nervous tomorrow.

2. If she delivers a good speech, she will receive a good grade.

   ____

   ____

3. What will happen if she forgets part of her speech?

   ____

4. She can look at her notes if she forgets part of her speech.

   ____

5. She will speak more confidently if she likes the topic.

   ____

6. If Kimberly practices in front of her friends, they can give her feedback.

   ____

7. She will do a better job if she sleeps well tonight.

   ____

8. If her speech is too long or too short, the teacher will lower her grade.

   ____

9. She can practice more if she has the time.

____

10. If Kimberly is more prepared, she can enjoy giving this speech.

____

5 Practice

Circle the letter that best describes the meaning of each sentence.

1. If Trisha runs fifty miles a week, she will be ready for the marathon.

   a. This may possibly happen. If she does the weekly running, she will definitely be ready. (a real conditional)

   b. This is a contrary-to-fact or unreal situation. She doesn't run fifty miles a week now. (an unreal conditional)

2. If Trisha won the marathon, she would get $10,000 in prize money.

   a. This may possibly happen. If she wins, she will definitely get $10,000 in prize money. (a real conditional)

   b. This is only a hypothetical situation. (an unreal conditional)

3. She would wear a brace on her knee if it started to hurt.

   a. This may possibly happen. If her knee does hurt, she will wear a brace. (a real conditional)

   b. This is a contrary-to-fact or unreal situation. Her knee doesn't hurt now, and isn't likely to hurt. (an unreal conditional)

4. On the day of the marathon, she would quit running if the weather were too hot.

   a. This may possibly happen. Maybe the weather has already been forecasted to be hot, so if it is really hot, she will quit running. (a real conditional)

   b. This is only a hypothetical situation. This is what she'd do if this were to happen. (an unreal conditional)

5. If Trisha's friends and family come to cheer her on, she'll be very happy.

   a. This may possibly happen. Maybe they live nearby, and if they do come to cheer her on, she will be happy. (a real conditional)

   b. This is an unreal situation. Trisha's friends and family aren't likely to come cheer her on (for whatever reason). (an unreal conditional)

6. While running the marathon, Trisha can stop at a water station if she gets thirsty.

   a. This may possibly happen. Trisha is likely to get thirsty; twenty-six miles is a long way to run! (a real conditional)

   b. This is a contrary-to-fact, hypothetical, or unreal situation. Trisha isn't likely to get thirsty. (an unreal conditional)

7. If she got lost while running the marathon, the race officials would help her to find her way back to the route.

   a. This may possibly happen. Maybe the route is not well-marked. (a real conditional)

   b. This is a contrary-to-fact, hypothetical, or unreal situation. She's not likely to get lost in a major race; the route is well-marked. (an unreal conditional)

8. Trisha couldn't run twenty-six miles if she didn't love running.

   a. This states that something is always true in a specific situation. (a real conditional)

   b. This states a contrary-to-fact condition. Trisha does love running. (an unreal conditional)

6 Practice

Write what you would or wouldn't do in each situation. Give a reason for your advice.

1. What would you do if you got lost while traveling in a city where you didn't speak the language? Why? ______________________

   ____

   ____

   ____

2. What would you do if you got a bill that you could not pay? Why?

   ____

   ____

   ____

   ____

3. What would you do if you saw someone cheating on a test? Why?

   ____

   ____

   ____

   ____

4. What would you do if your house or building caught on fire? Why?

____

____

____

____

5. What would you do if you were Kimberly (from Practice 4) and you had to give a speech? Why?

____

____

____

____

14c Unreal Conditional Sentences in the Past; Mixed Conditional Sentences

Student Book p. 422

7 Practice

Read the sentences. Rewrite them as unreal conditional sentences in the past or as mixed conditional sentences. Use the modals in parentheses for the main clause.

1. Raymond learned to ride a bike at an early age. He is such an excellent bicycle messenger today. (would not)

If Raymond hadn't learned to ride a bike at an early age, he wouldn't be such an excellent bicycle messenger today.

2. Raymond's uncle owned a bike messenger company. Raymond got a job there. (might not)

____

____

3. Last week, Raymond talked on his cell phone while riding. He got hit by a car. (would not)

____

____

4. He was busy talking. He didn't hear the car behind him. (could)

____

____

5. He was late meeting a customer. He called to apologize. (would not)

____

____

6. The car was going slowly. Therefore, Raymond was not badly injured. (could)

____

____

7. Because Raymond's boss is his uncle, Raymond wasn't fired from his job. (might)

____

____

8. Raymond isn't afraid to ride his bike in traffic. He returned to work yesterday. (could not)

____

____

8 Practice

Reread the sentences you wrote in Practice 7. Write *UP* if the sentence is an unreal conditional sentence in the past. Write *M* if the sentence is a mixed conditional.

1. _____
2. _____
3. _____
4. _____
5. _____
6. _____
7. _____
8. _____

9 Practice

Complete the sentences with either conditional or main clauses and your own ideas. Use past unreal conditionals or mixed conditionals. Use *might (not), could (not),* or *would (not)* in the main clause.

1. If I hadn't come to this class, ______________________________.
2. ______________________________ if I hadn't studied English.
3. My parents would have been very happy ______________________________.
4. My parents wouldn't have been so happy ______________________________.
5. English would be easier to learn ______________________________.
6. I might not have needed this book ______________________________.
7. ______________________________ if I had paid more attention in class.
8. The teacher would be angry ______________________________.

14d Conditional Sentences with *As If* and *As Though*

Student Book p. 426

10 Practice

Read the sentences. Write *R* next to the sentence if it expresses a real situation. Write *U* if it expresses an unreal situation.

_____ 1. You look as though you're worried about something.

_____ 2. My coworker is acting as if she were the boss.

_____ 3. You talk as if you had already gotten the job.

_____ 4. You talk as though you already have the job.

_____ 5. My boss sounds as if she will leave her position soon.

_____ 6. It seems like my coworker wanted to quit.

11 Practice

Read the sentences. Rewrite the real conditional sentences as unreal, using the simple past or past perfect tense. Rewrite the unreal conditional sentences as real, using the simple present, *be going to,* or *will.* Remember to make changes to the first verb in the sentence as necessary.

1. You look as though you didn't sleep last night.

   You look as though you are tired.

2. It looks as if the sun is going to come out soon.

   ____

3. She talks as if she got the job.

   ____

4. The band sounded like they hadn't practiced.

   ____

5. It looks as though we'll have too much food for the party.

   ____

6. It looks as if there's a big party down the hall.

   ____

7. You look like you know how to solve the problem.

   ____

8. His mother sounded as if she were angry about something.

   ____

12 Practice

Look at the photos. What do you think has happened? What do you think is going to happen? Write two sentences about each photo. Use *as if, as though,* or *like.*

A.

1. *It looks as though the man isn't going to be hurt.*
2. *It looks as if the bicycle tires have slipped in the sand.*

B.

1. ______________________________
____
____

2. ______________________________
____
____

C.

1. ______________________________
____
____
____

2. ______________________________
____
____
____

D.

1. ______________________________
____
____
____

2. ______________________________
____
____
____

14e Conditional Sentences Without *If*

Student Book p. 428

13 Practice

Rewrite the sentences in two ways as conditional sentences without *if*. The first time, use inverted subject-verb word order. The second time, use an implied conditional and the words in parentheses.

1. If Matthew had known his parents were coming to visit, he would have cleaned his apartment.

   a. Had Matthew known his parents were coming to visit, he would have cleaned his apartment.

   b. (otherwise)

   Matthew didn't know his parents were coming to visit. Otherwise, he would have cleaned his apartment.

2. If he had had more time, he would have washed the dishes in the sink.

   a. ______________________

   b. (with)

   ____

3. If his mother should see the stains on the rug, she will be upset.

   a. ______________________

   b. (might / if so)

   ____

4. If his friend hadn't helped him, he wouldn't have finished cleaning in time.

   a. ______________________

b. (without)

____

____

5. If the hotels hadn't been full this weekend, they wouldn't have asked to stay with Matthew.

a. ____

____

b. (otherwise)

____

____

6. If Matthew's parents should arrive early, they'll take him out to dinner.

a. ____

____

b. (might / if so)

____

____

14 Practice

Read the letter of complaint. Rewrite the selected sentences as conditional sentences with *if*.

To the Stimson Luggage Company:

I am returning a suitcase that I purchased from your company. I have only used it once, on a recent trip to France. Had I known that the suitcase would break so easily, (1) I never would have bought it. First of all, the handle broke at the airport. Had the handle not broken, (2) I wouldn't have had to travel around France with a rope tied to the suitcase.

In addition to the broken handle, the zipper broke—even though I had only used it five times. It's true that were my suitcase not so full, (3) the zipper might not have broken. However, your company advertises the SuperStrong zipper. Your ad says that should the suitcase get too full, (4) the zipper will not break. Had the zipper not broken, (5)

I wouldn't have lost some of my clothing.

Also, the outside pocket ripped. I didn't realize the fabric was so thin. Otherwise, I
6
wouldn't have put anything in there.

Were I you, I would carefully test my product before giving false information
7
about it.

I would like my money refunded. I have enclosed my sales slip. I hope your company improves its products in the future. If so, I will consider buying another
8
Stimson suitcase. Until then, however, I will look for another brand.

Sincerely,

Debra Johnson

1. ______________________________

____

2. ______________________________

____

3. ______________________________

____

4. ______________________________

____

5. ______________________________

____

6. ______________________________

____

7. ______________________________

____

8. ______________________________

____

14f Wishes About the Present, Future, and Past; *Hope*

Student Book p. 432

15 Practice

Match the following wishes with the types of wishes.

Types of Wishes
a. Regret about the past
b. A wish for something to change or stop (and that probably won't happen)
c. A wish for something to be different in the present and future
d. A desire for a possible real situation

_____ **1.** I hope I find a job soon. I applied for ten jobs last week!

_____ **2.** I wish I hadn't spent all my money last weekend. Now I don't have any left to go out with my friends this weekend.

_____ **3.** I wish my sister would stop asking to borrow money. I don't have any to give her.

_____ **4.** I can't save money easily. I wish I could save money as well as my brother.

16 Practice

Luis is trying to do a homework assignment. Write his wishes. You may use or omit *that*. There may be more than one way to rewrite some sentences.

1. Luis doesn't have a computer at home.

He wishes he had a computer at home.

2. He has to use the library computer.

____

____

3. The Internet connection is slow.

____

____

4. He can only use the computer for thirty minutes. ______________________________

____

5. His friend Joe is telling him jokes. ______________________________

____

6. He can't print on the library computer. ______________________________

____

7. He left his floppy disk at home. ______________________________

____

8. He forgot one of his books. ______________________________

____

9. He lost his library card. ______________________________

____

10. He can't finish the assignment. ______________________________

____

17 Practice

Luis is feeling better about the following situations. Change his negative thoughts to positive thoughts by rewriting the sentences. Rewrite the unreal situations as possible real situations using *hope*. You may use or omit *that*.

1. I don't have enough time to finish the assignment. I wish I had more time.

   The library is open for thirty more minutes. I hope I have enough time to finish the assignment.

2. The librarian is busy. I wish she could help me.

   Now she seems to be free. ______________________________

3. I wish I could buy my own computer. They're so expensive.

   I saw a sign in the library. Someone is selling a used computer. ______________________________

   ____

4. I wish that my friend had written down the assignment, but he almost never does that.

   I saw my friend writing something down in class. ______________________________

   ____

5. I wish that people would stop talking. It's so loud!

   The librarian just told people to be quiet. ______________________________

   ____

6. I wish I had brought money for the photocopy machine. I forgot it.

   I hear some change in the bottom of my bag. ______________________________

   ____

18 Practice

Write wishes about your job, school, or class.

1. Write four things you wish were different about your job, school, or class right now.

   ____

   ____

   ____

   ____

   ____

2. Write four things you wish hadn't happened at your job, school, or class in the past.

   ____

   ____

   ____

   ____

   ____

3. Write four hopes you have about your job, school, or class.

   ____

   ____

   ____

   ____

   ____

14g Conditional Sentences with *If Only*

Student Book p. 434

19 Practice

Miguel is looking for a job. Write wishes for him using *if only*. Pay attention to the verb tense.

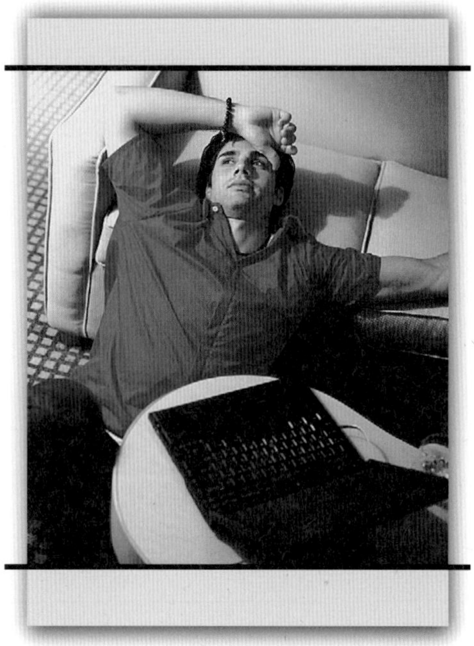

1. Miguel doesn't have a job right now. He thinks,

   "If only I had a job right now."

2. Miguel doesn't have an MBA. He thinks,

   "______________________________________

   ______________________________________."

3. He has to work near his home. He thinks,

   "______________________________________

   ______________________________________."

4. He doesn't like to wear suits.

   "______________________________________

   ______________________________________."

5. He didn't finish college. "______________________________________."

6. He can't work on weekends. "______________________________________

   ______________________________________."

7. He never learned to use a lot of computer programs. "______________________________________

   ______________________________________."

8. A job that he wanted was given to someone else. "______________________________________

   ______________________________________."

9. He doesn't have a suit to wear to a job interview. "______________________________________

   ______________________________________."

10. He didn't start looking for jobs until last week. "______________________________

____."

11. He is late paying the rent this month. "______________________________

____."

12. He lost his job last month. "______________________________

____."

20 Practice

Write six regrets you have about choices you made in the past. Use *if only* and the past perfect.

Examples: *If only I had seen the dentist more often! Then I wouldn't have so many problems with my teeth.*

If only I hadn't taken Route 128! Then I wouldn't have been stuck in traffic for two hours.

____

____

____

____

____

____

____

____

____

____

____

____

SELF-TEST

A Choose the best answer, A, B, C, or D, to complete the sentence. Mark your answer by darkening the oval with the same letter.

1. The movie might not have been so popular if a famous actor ____________ in it.

A. wasn't (A) (B) (C) (D)
B. wouldn't have been
C. isn't
D. hadn't been

2. It is getting cold outside. It feels ____________ it's going to snow.

A. like if (A) (B) (C) (D)
B. as if
C. though
D. though if

3. I wish I ____________ you with the homework assignment, but I don't understand it.

A. could help (A) (B) (C) (D)
B. should help
C. would help
D. would have helped

4. I didn't read that chapter. ____________, I would have understood the lecture.

A. Had I read it (A) (B) (C) (D)
B. If I read it
C. I had read it
D. If had I read it

5. If you ____________ to the supermarket on your way home, please pick up some milk.

A. went (A) (B) (C) (D)
B. will go
C. would have gone
D. should go

6. If only I ____________ a week, I could have bought that MP3 player on sale.

A. waited (A) (B) (C) (D)
B. had waited
C. would have waited
D. would had waited

7. I wouldn't shop there if I ____________ you. That store is too expensive.

A. was (A) (B) (C) (D)
B. will be
C. were
D. had been

8. Joe is overweight. He wishes that he ____________ some weight.

A. lost (A) (B) (C) (D)
B. can lose
C. could lose
D. could lost

9. Please give this book to Mary if you ____________ her tonight.

A. see (A) (B) (C) (D)
B. would see
C. had seen
D. will see

10. Everyone ____________ the test if the teacher had given it today.

A. might had failed (A) (B) (C) (D)
B. might have failed
C. might fail
D. might failed

B Find the underlined word or phrase, A, B, C, or D, that is incorrect. Mark your answer by darkening the oval with the same letter.

1. Before going (A) on a road trip, I would check (B) the oil in your car if (C) I am (D) you.

   Ⓐ Ⓑ Ⓒ Ⓓ

2. If you will direct (A) the sunlight to paper (B) with a magnifying glass (C), the paper will burn (D).

   Ⓐ Ⓑ Ⓒ Ⓓ

3. If only (A) we didn't stay up (B) so late, we wouldn't (C) have missed (D) our morning class.

   Ⓐ Ⓑ Ⓒ Ⓓ

4. What (A) you will do (B) if (C) you should have (D) a problem with your car?

   Ⓐ Ⓑ Ⓒ Ⓓ

5. We were (A) so hungry that we ate (B) like if (C) we would never see (D) food again.

   Ⓐ Ⓑ Ⓒ Ⓓ

6. Where will (A) you go (B) if you could travel (C) anywhere in the world (D)?

   Ⓐ Ⓑ Ⓒ Ⓓ

7. Elizabeth doesn't have a car. She wishes (A) that (B) she doesn't have (C) to take (D) the subway to work every day.

   Ⓐ Ⓑ Ⓒ Ⓓ

8. If I had been (A) paid (B) today, I could had (C) bought (D) that new bag.

   Ⓐ Ⓑ Ⓒ Ⓓ

9. I don't like to be (A) around Beth because she always sounds (B) though (C) she's having (D) a bad day.

   Ⓐ Ⓑ Ⓒ Ⓓ

10. My friend might go (A) to college if (B) his high school teachers had encouraged (C) him (D) to.

    Ⓐ Ⓑ Ⓒ Ⓓ